Reinventing
Mom

Reinventing
Mom

SEVEN PATHWAYS TO BECOMING THE MOM
AND WOMAN YOU ARE MEANT TO BE

Kelly Pryde, Ph.D.

iUniverse LLC
Bloomington

REINVENTING MOM
Seven Pathways to Becoming the Mom and Woman You Are Meant to Be

iUniverse books may be ordered through booksellers or by contacting:

iUniverse LLC
1663 Liberty Drive
Bloomington, IN 47403
www.iuniverse.com
1-800-Authors (1-800-288-4677)

Because of the dynamic nature of the Internet, any web addresses or links contained in this book may have changed since publication and may no longer be valid. The views expressed in this work are solely those of the author and do not necessarily reflect the views of the publisher, and the publisher hereby disclaims any responsibility for them.

Certain stock imagery © Thinkstock.

ISBN: 978-1-4917-1211-5 (sc)
ISBN: 978-1-4917-1210-8 (e)

Library of Congress Control Number: 2013919548

Printed in the United States of America.

Grateful acknowledgment is made for permission to quote or adapt the following:
Excerpt from Women's Bodies, Women's Wisdom, by Christiane Northrup, M.D. Copyright 2010. Published by Bantam Dell, New York. Used by permission of the author; excerpt from the poem "The Invitation," by Oriah Mountain Dreamer from The Invitation. Copyright 1999. Published by HarperOne, San Francisco. Used by permission of the author; excerpt from The Call, by Oriah Mountain Dreamer. Copyright 2003. Published by HarperOne, San Francisco. Used by permission of the author; adaptation of "The Good Life Parable," by Mark Albion from More Than Money. Copyright 2008. Published by BK Life, San Francisco. Used by permission of the author; adaptation of "Mrs. Judgy McJudgerson at the Mall," by Julie Cole from YummyMummyClub.ca Blog. Copyright 2011. Published by YummyMummyClub.ca. Used by permission of the author.

Author's note: Many of the names and stories in this book are composites. Unless indicated by both first and last names, names and identifying characteristics have been changed to respect confidentiality. Nevertheless, the stories reflect real situations in the lives of the hundreds of Moms I have worked with over the years.

CONTENTS

PART THREE
Staying the Path

"Your children will become what you are;
so be what you want them to be."
—David Bly

Part One

A New Approach to Life and Motherhood

INTRODUCTION

The "Running on Empty" Phenomenon

It was a typical Monday morning at our house. I was scrambling to get my five-year-old ready to catch her bus for school, my two-year-old ready for daycare, and myself ready for a 9 A.M. appointment. For the third time in the last two minutes, I called out, "C'mon guys! Get your shoes on!" I quickly glanced at my watch—five minutes until the bus came.

I scrambled to fill the backpacks and help my daughter tie her shoes when all of a sudden I heard the sound of water spilling on the floor. My two-year-old had dumped the dog's water bowl . . . AGAIN! A few choice words went through my head and I felt my blood pressure rise as I rushed over to prevent any further disaster. I conveniently found a towel from one of the several baskets of dirty laundry nearby and threw it down on the puddle. Three minutes until the bus.

I scooped up my son and rushed back to the front door to get his shoes on. In a full-blown frenzy at that point, I strapped the last piece of Velcro on his shoe and shouted, "C'mon guys, let's move! We're gonna miss the bus!" I grabbed the backpacks and ushered everyone out the door to head down to the bus stop.

As we began our walk down the street, I let out a sigh of relief knowing that we were going to make it on time. My five-year-old daughter (who I swear is a therapist-in-training sometimes!) unexpectedly patted me on the arm and said, "Don't worry, Mom. Everything's fine." "Thanks honey," I said with a smile. "Mommy just gets frazzled sometimes when we're running late." With a puzzled look on her face, she asked me what "frazzled" meant. "Oh, that just means I'm worn out and need to recharge my batteries," I explained. She turned to me shaking her head and said, "Mom, I don't think your batteries are the rechargeable kind!"

If you're a Mom whose ever felt like your batteries are not the rechargeable kind, then you've picked up the right book. From being on-demand 24/7 and juggling children, home management, work, relationships, and the never-ending to-do lists, Moms are constantly performing superhuman feats of multitasking while we take care of others. We strive to do the invincible and we are definitely in need of recharging—in more ways than one.

Up until a few years ago, I thought this perpetual state of busyness and the frazzled feelings that went along with it were just part and parcel of being a Mom. After all, other Moms I knew claimed to be in the same boat and I remembered my own Mom feeling this way much of the time. Heck, even writer and first-time Mom, Lisa Kogan, wrote in *O, The Oprah Magazine* that "mommy time" is a myth and that all the Moms she knew were "in serious need of a haircut and a shot of caffeine." It seemed like being a worn out Mom-on-the-go was *just the way things are.*

But there was something about this "way" that didn't sit well with me. And the day that I was so physically and emotionally drained that the thought of making dinner for my five- and two-year old was too overwhelming that I had to order pizza, I decided that this "way" is anything but normal. This "way" was robbing me of my energy and happiness and it was preventing me from being the Mom and person that I wanted to be. This "way" had to go.

> **I am woman. I am invincible. I am tired.**
> —ANONYMOUS

But what was the alternative? The "I-can-do-it-all" supermom approach clearly didn't work—I had been on the verge of burn-out more times than I cared to count. I tried taking "mommy time" only to find that the issues I was dealing with were still there waiting for me when I got back. I knew there must be a better way of doing things.

That's when it occurred to me: it was the *doing* that was the problem. This "way" that didn't work was a result of the constant doing and striving—to do more and have more for ourselves and our children, and, above all else, to *be* more.

It was an "Aha" moment.

THIS "WAY"—THE PROBLEM THAT HAS A NAME

In her bestselling book *Perfect Madness: Motherhood in the Age of Anxiety*, Judith Warner explores an "existential discomfort" facing today's young mothers. She describes a "caught-by-the-throat feeling" mothers have of always doing something wrong and of struggling to find their way through all of the pressure, stress, and worry they contend with on a daily basis.

In probably the most poignant and compelling paragraph of the book, Warner states: "This feeling—this widespread, choking cocktail of guilt and anxiety and resentment and regret—is poisoning motherhood for . . . women today. Lowering our horizons and limiting our minds. Sapping energy that we should have for ourselves and our children. And drowning out thoughts that might lead us, collectively, to formulate solutions."

After years of research and listening to hundreds of mothers describe this feeling, Warner discovered that this problem was such an overwhelming, messy mix of things that none of the women could name it. It remained as pioneering feminist Betty Friedan described decades earlier in her seminal book *The Feminine Mystique*, "the problem that has no name."

I know this feeling. It was the same feeling I had the day I was so exhausted and overwhelmed that I couldn't make dinner for my kids. It was the same feeling I used to have on my daily commute taking my kids to daycare and going to a job that was sucking the life out of me. It was the feeling that this "way" of living and parenting wasn't working. Chances are you know this feeling too. But I believe this feeling—this widespread, messy problem—does have a name. It's called *running on empty*.

Running on Empty

Running on empty is a way of living that is characterized by a state of *depletion* and *disconnection*. The depletion occurs at our physical, emotional, and spiritual levels of being—we feel frazzled, worn out, moody, underappreciated, and unhappy. The disconnection occurs from our inner selves and our sense of what's real and important in our lives. Regardless of how educated, talented, and successful we might be, this depleted and disconnected way of living affects all groups of Moms.

While running on empty has many unique faces, there are several common issues that Moms experience:

- Feeling stressed out and frazzled much of the time—you always seem to be "on-the-go" and/or life feels like one big "to-do" list.
- Feeling like you never have any time for yourself.
- Emotional exhaustion, feeling like you have nothing left to give.
- Being irritable and moody more often than you'd like.
- Feeling guilty about not being the Mom you want to be.
- Frequently comparing yourself to other Moms and worrying that they're doing a better job than you.
- Having low levels of physical energy. (Exercise? Yeah, right!)
- Feeling resentful that nobody looks after *your* needs.
- Sensing an uncertain sadness, like something is missing in your life.

Almost all of us experience these feelings in our lives as Moms—you, me, our neighbors, the Moms at playgroup, the Moms in the boardroom, the Moms at soccer. Many of us manage to put on a smile and portray some semblance of togetherness, but if we're honest with ourselves, we know these feelings are there. It is the "way" of motherhood in our culture. And even though millions of Moms struggle with these issues everyday, this running on empty way of life is certainly not normal, or healthy.

Being a mother can be fraught with tension. I definitely relate to the frantic fear that you're screwing up.
—Julia Louis-Dreyfus

I know from personal experience and from my experiences with countless other Moms I've worked with over the years that running on empty can lead to a number of emotional and physical health issues over time. Initially, we experience many of the symptoms described above—stress, fatigue, moodiness, and sadness. This is our body and soul's way of telling us that something in our life is out of sorts. If we don't listen and make the necessary changes, the symptoms persist and then worsen in an attempt to get our attention. We get headaches, sleep problems, high blood pressure, or more extreme fatigue. If we continue to ignore the warning signals, our bodies and souls begin to shout as a last resort with more serious problems such as heart disease, exhaustion, or depression.

And just how well are we tuned in to what our bodies and souls are trying to tell us? Current research tells us that heart disease is *the* major health risk facing women today. More than thirty percent of women in their child-rearing years have symptoms of depression according to Mental Health America. And a recent survey by the American Psychological Association reports that women's stress—including physical and emotional symptoms such as fatigue, lack of energy, headaches, and wanting to cry—is on the rise.

It's clear that we are not listening.

We don't get adequate nutrition or activity for our female bodies and we don't take sufficient downtime to recharge. We run on adrenaline and put too much pressure on ourselves to get everything done *and* be great at it. We have learned to tune out our intuition—our powerful internal sense of what is right for us and our families. And we sacrifice our inner selves with all of our dreams and passions in the name of attending to everyone else's needs.

Our bodies and souls are insistently calling to us and we are not listening. We're caught up in this "way," too busy *doing* and too tired to notice.

HOW DID WE GET HERE?

I don't believe for a second that we have consciously chosen this running on empty lifestyle—we are smart, talented, capable women. How is it then that so many of us are caught up in it? I believe there are several factors that account for how we got here and why we run on empty: our culture, our personal histories, and our female biology.

Any day that ends up with you dangling by a slender psychic thread should prompt the very valid question "How the Bloody Hell Did I Get Here?"

—Sarah Ban Breathnach

Our Culture: The Whirlwind of Motherhood

For hundreds of years, motherhood and the concept of "good mothering" has been a cultural invention. And if we consider the culture we live and parent in today, it isn't any wonder that we're all running on empty.

We live in an incredibly busy world filled with noise, speed, and activity. From our workplaces and schools, to television and the internet, to books, magazines, and advertising, we are surrounded by the constant chatter of messages about success and "being our best." And motherhood is no exception.

Pick up any parenting or women's magazine in the grocery checkout aisle and you'll see the same message: "Five foods that will make your child smarter;" "How to lose that baby weight in twenty days;" "Ten tips for being a stress-free Mom;" "Secrets of mommy millionaires;" "Two-minute techniques for connecting with your kids."

Smarter, thinner, calmer, richer, happier—the message our culture leads us to believe is clear: *we need more in order to be more.* At a deep level, many of us are longing for that something more so much—so worried about not doing enough and being enough—that we unconsciously buy into the message and push ourselves to the limits trying to do more and better and best for ourselves and for our children.

And it is certainly easy for us in today's world to look outside of ourselves and find more. During the last 100 years, the rise of scientific and psychological advances in parenting and child development has led to an overwhelming amount of how-to information for mothers. Experts tell us the best ways to feed, soothe, sleep, protect, teach, play, nurture, and speak to our children. While these advances have led to many positive changes, the sheer volume and convenience of this information has come at a cost. Not only has it fanned our fears and anxieties about doing all the right things and doing what's best for our children, but it has also drowned out that gentle voice within us causing us to doubt ourselves and disconnect from our maternal wisdom and intuition.

With all of these cultural influences and pressures, the "good mother" today is caught in a kind of whirlwind. She is overly busy, anxious, and overwhelmed trying to live up to all of the standards and expectations placed on her. At the same time, she feels guilty and inadequate that she can't keep up. And the faster she goes, the further behind she falls.

> **If you are going in the wrong direction, speeding up doesn't help.**
>
> —MICHAEL ANNISON, *Managing the Whirlwind*

By far, this lifestyle is one of the biggest factors depleting us of our physical, emotional, and spiritual well-being. The ironic thing is, this lifestyle—this "whirlwind," this "way"—is also fueled to a large extent by ourselves . . .

The Evolution of Modern Motherhood

HOW CULTURE INVENTS THE "GOOD MOTHER"

Motherhood as we know it today has evolved from a series of cultural trends over the last 100 years—trends that have defined and influenced our idea of the "good mother." Take a look . . .

- **Scientific Mom (1900-1940)** With the rise in science and psychology, the good mother follows "strict principles of scientific parenting." Constant vigilance, emotional distance, and perfect monitoring of food and activities are required to maintain health and prevent psychological harm.
- **Sacrificial Mom (1940-1970)** The cold, scientific approach takes a 180° turn to a cuddly, 24/7 child-centered approach. The good mother is ever-present and all-providing—she stimulates cognitive development and anticipates her child's every need, all while feeling personally fulfilled. (Remember June Cleaver?!) But with her increase in education and involvement in the workforce, the good mother begins to crave a life of her own.
- **Supermom (1970-1990)** With the women's lib movement, the good mother is able to have a career of her own and be a happier, healthier Mom at the same time. She can have it all! With increased choice and self-empowerment, the good mother becomes a model of non-stop high-performance at work and at home.

- **Millennial Mom (1990-Present)** A shift occurs that brings children's self-esteem to the cultural forefront. A child-centered focus combined with women's self-empowerment leads the good mother to become a hipper, more high-tech blend of her maternal predecessors—"übermom." Whether at home, in the workplace, or building her own business, Mom is hyper-aware and hyper-connected as she juggles everything from motherhood and personal ambition to social media and eco-friendly living.

Source: Thurer, S. (1995). The Myths of Motherhood: How Culture Reinvents the Good Mother. *New York: Penguin*

Our Personal Histories: An Inconvenient Truth

Okay, Oprah and Dr. Phil have been around long enough for us to know that we have unresolved issues. It's a fact and just a natural part of life. We all have emotional "stuff" that we carry around with us. We carry it in our thoughts, we take it into our relationships, and it drives a lot of our behavior—whether we recognize it or not and whether we like it our not. And the often messy, unpleasant nature of these emotional issues makes it an inconvenient truth for many.

I remember life coach Cheryl Richardson once describing how we acquire all of this emotional "stuff" in a lecture she gave at Mile Hi Church in Colorado. She gave the analogy of each of us coming into the world as a beautiful work of art—a unique and wonderful painting. She went on to explain that over time our painting starts to get tarnished—dirt gets thrown it, food is dumped on it, it gets stepped on, it's not always given the gentle care it needs. The painting is blurred and gradually becomes so obscured by all of the "stuff" that has built up on it over the years that it becomes disconnected from that original, genuine work of art.

I love this analogy. It aptly describes our personal histories and how we acquire all of the messy emotional issues in our lives. We don't ask for them, they are thrown at us—usually by unconscious intent from others who have their own emotional issues. Because of the messy and confusing and inconvenient nature of these issues, it is often easier to mask all the stuff on our work of art rather than properly clean and restore it to its original brilliance. We throw on a great pair of shoes, some new furniture, or a high-powered job and we try to carry on.

And then our children are born.

Children have the magical effect of bringing all of our emotional stuff to the surface. They remind us of all the things we wish had or hadn't happened to us in our own childhood. And because we love them fiercely and want so much for them to be happy and successful, we vow that we won't let those things happen to them. We're going to do things differently. And better.

As a result, we begin to compensate for the various forms of lack and disappointment we experienced as children. We tell our kids how "good" they are and what "good jobs" they do at *every* possible opportunity. We try to be physically present and mentally engaged with them as much as possible. We hover over them with a hyper-awareness of their emotional needs so that we can be there for them—more perfectly than perhaps our own parents were. And when we can't be there perfectly, which is most always, we feel incredibly guilty and we worry about the ripple effects of our less-than-ideal actions on their well-being.

At the end of the day, much of what we expend a great deal of our energy on is "re-parenting" our own selves and trying to protect what we perceive as the ever-so-fragile emotional lives of our children. We fuel the whirlwind of motherhood with our fears of emotional shortcomings and our expectations of emotional goodness, and we exhaust ourselves of energy that we could have for ourselves and our children by trying to mask all of these insecurities. We're disconnected from that original and genuine work of art.

> **Harboring dark secrets. Lying. Pretending. Trying to be some-one you're not. All these things are weights that prevent you from reaching your highest potential. In order to fly, you have to get the weight, the garbage off of your wings.**
>
> —Oprah Winfrey

Our Female Biology: Wired to Tend

On top of our success-driven culture and our personal histories, the very nature of being female contributes to the whirlwind of motherhood.

We all know about "fight or flight"—our primitive and automatic built-in response that enables us to deal with stressful situations. For years we learned that stress from internal worry or external circumstance causes our body to shift into a state of arousal. Our alertness intensifies, adrenaline fuels our muscles and limbs, our perception of pain diminishes, our rational thinking is disengaged, and fear becomes the lens through which we see the world. We become ready to "fight" or "flee." Or do we?

It turns out there's more to this story than we initially understood, especially as it applies to us Moms.

Prior to 1995, only about seventeen percent of participants in stress studies were women! Because of that, much of how we understood and managed stress was based on studies of men. Fortunately, over the last decade we have learned a lot more about how women respond to stress as well. Although we experience the same state of arousal as men do, we don't appear to have the same "fight or flight" instinct men have when it comes to our family. Because we are fundamentally a nurturant species, in times of stress a mother's instinct is to "tend."

That's right. When we are faced with stressful situations, our bodies shift into overdrive, rational thought goes out the window, and we tend to everybody's needs. Doesn't that explain so much?!

These findings on women and stress come from the groundbreaking work of UCLA professor and psychologist Shelley Taylor. In her book, *The Tending Instinct*, Taylor pulls together research from evolutionary science, biology, and social psychology to explain how the unique blend of hormones in women—hormones such as oxytocin and estrogen—work together in such a way that they lead us to tend and protect our children and family members at all costs. In this way, the tending instinct is a built-in survival response that will often drive us to selfless behaviors. It is the biological imperative that causes us to put ourselves at great risk if it means protecting the life of our child.

> **Oh what a power is mother-hood, possessing**
> **A potent spell**
> **All women alike**
> **Fight fiercely for a child.**
> —EURIPEDES

This tending response is essential to human nature. It offers protection for young children and enhances the physical and emotional well-being of everyone around us. As Taylor points out, "Across stressful and non-stressful times and across the lifespan, we all benefit from women's tending." Everyone except Mom, that is.

Because of our hectic lifestyles and the 24/7 demands and expectations upon us as mothers, we spend much of our time in a state of arousal—the stressed out kind, that is! As a result, our tending instincts have run amok and we are running around selflessly tending and nurturing and *doing* for everyone else at a cost to our own physical, emotional, and spiritual well-being—running on empty.

IT'S TIME FOR A NEW WAY

We can have the best time-management organizer on the market, a prioritized to-do list, a personal trainer, a nanny, a housekeeper. We can delegate, take courses, and read all the self-help books we can muster on how to find that perfect and ever-so-elusive life balance. The truth is: The more external factors we introduce into our lives, the more inconsistency, complexity, and stress we experience. We don't need *more*. And we certainly don't need a better or more efficient way of *doing* things.

For the last 100 years, the "good mother" has tried different ways of doing things by subscribing to the cultural trend of the time—the cold, scientific approach, the sacrificial happy housewife approach, the Supermom approach, the Soccer Mom approach, the work-at-home approach. But no matter how much we have changed the external conditions of our lives, our inner experiences have remained the same. Just like our maternal predecessors, we are tired, worried, and unhappy—feeling like something is just not right, that something is missing.

Your quality of life is not determined by what you add to it, but by what you take away from it.

—CHERYL RICHARDSON

The Mommy Diaries

WE'RE ALL IN THE SAME BOAT

Although much has changed over the years, we actually share many of the same running on empty feelings as our maternal predecessors . . .

"I am constantly worried about whether or not I'm doing or saying the right thing . . . I feel pushed and pulled. Most of the time I'm under terrible pressure."

"I have no time for myself, no life of my own."

"I don't know why I should be so tired . . . . I just don't feel alive."

—Mothers quoted in *Redbook*, 1960

I fear I cannot love enough or in the right way or in the right amounts . . . That I am not providing the home life I wanted to have when I was growing up."

"Four years into mommyhood, my energy had waned, as had my self-esteem . . . . My day was booked in service to my kids, each day, every day, relentless."

—Mothers quoted in *Perfect Madness*, 2006

Ironically, the one thing we have rarely done through the various evolutions of motherhood is consult ourselves. I don't mean our immediate surface selves where our thoughts, judgments, and to-do lists reside, but our deeper, inner Selves where our feelings, insights, and passions live. We have forgotten how to do that. We have become so externally-focused that we have disconnected from our inner Selves and forgotten how to listen to that all-knowing voice within us.

It is the thinking and doing without this inner awareness that is the main dilemma of motherhood and the running on empty phenomenon. It is the *something* that is missing.

Unless we learn to reconnect with our inner Selves and become consciously aware of what our bodies and souls are telling us, no amount of organizing, planning, shopping, achieving, running around, or doing will help. We will continue to run on empty and be disconnected from what is real and important in our lives and in the lives of our children.

MEANWHILE, BACK ON THE COUCH . . .

As I lay on my couch that day feeling depleted and guilty while my kids ate pizza and watched movies, I decided a new "way" was in order. Out of my frustration and despair with this running on empty lifestyle, the idea for reinvention was born.

As you will learn throughout this book, reinvention is not about a quick-fix makeover nor is it about some kind of "mom revolution." Rather, it is about a kind of evolution. It's about redefining how we think about and go about our roles as Moms. It's about disconnecting from all of the expectations and judgments and shoulds and reconnecting with who we really are and what matters to us as unique individuals. And it's about the exhilarating journey towards being the Moms and women *we are meant to be*—for ourselves and for our children.

> **The people who get on in this world are the people who get up and look for the circumstances they want, and, if they can't find them, make them.**
>
> —George Bernard Shaw

As we begin to reconnect with our inner Selves, we start to connect with our outer lives with greater energy, wisdom, purpose, and joy. When we're able to do that for ourselves, we can then help our children do the same. I believe this is one of the greatest gifts we can give them.

HOW THIS BOOK CAN HELP YOU

If you're like most Moms I know, you might be thinking "Yeah, yeah. I've heard just about all the mommy advice I can handle" or "Ugh, I don't have the time or energy for trying to change my life." This is the voice of the "running on empty Mom" talking and it is the biggest challenge I face in doing this work—most Moms are too tired and overextended to *do* one more thing. And let me tell you, I have been there, done that. There have been, and still are, many occasions where I've had a few choice words for the expert who "strongly recommends" or tells me what I "should" be doing. For me, these moments have become the warning signals indicating that some part of my life is running on empty and it's time to refuel. Nevertheless, these feelings are very real and it is hard to take action when you're depleted.

All I can tell you is this: I did not write this book to tell you how you *should* be living and parenting or to give you a step-by-step program that you *have to* follow in order to be a better Mom. There is no formula or set of guidelines for being a Mom that I can offer you. This is *your* life and these are *your* children. No one can listen to the whispers of your heart the way you can. No one can understand the tears, laughter, and needs of your children the way you can. Only you can determine what is right for you and your family—on your own terms in your own unique way.

What I can offer you is a new way of thinking about your role as Mom and how you can begin to reconnect with that inner wisdom that is insistently calling to you and trying to guide you in your unique life. Throughout the book, I have included many ideas, practices, explanations, and experiences from my own life and the lives of other Moms that will hopefully inspire you and help you on your journey.

Having embraced the process of reinvention in my own life, I can tell you that it does require effort and it is not always easy. But the gifts you receive in exchange are more than worth it. The various pathways of reinvention have and continue to help me discover who I am, how I feel, and how I want to live and parent. Although it

> **If it wasn't hard, everyone would do it. It's the hard that makes it great.**
>
> —TOM HANKS

is certainly not perfect, it certainly is joyful. I do know that. While I'd love to say I embrace the reinvention ideas and practices everyday, the reality is that I am still learning and I do find myself running on empty every now and again. The one thing I have learned is that tuning in and reconnecting to what my body and soul are telling me directs me where I need to go every time.

* * * * *

One of my favorite things to tell Moms is this: *You already have everything you need to be the Mom and woman you're meant to be—you just have to connect with it.* I hope this book will inspire and help you to do that.

REDEFINING MOTHERHOOD

A Framework for Reinvention

mother, *n. & v.* **n. 1** *a female parent.* **2** *a woman exercising control, influence, or authority like that of a mother.* **3** *(often cap.) a term of address for a female parent.* **v. 4** *to perform the tasks or duties of a female parent.*

If you look up the term "mother" in various dictionaries, these are the most common definitions that are given. I have to believe the individuals who came up with these very functional descriptions were not mothers! I think most of us would agree that our role as Mom goes much, much deeper than what is described here. But just how would we define what it means to be "Mom"?

Think about that for a moment. *What exactly does it mean to you to be "Mom"?*

When I ask Moms this question, they usually respond with a puzzled look and say: "Hmmm . . . that's a good question. I never really thought about that before."

I never really thought about that before.

How did we get this far in the world's most important job without knowing what it means to be Mom, without being able to define it? Don't get me wrong, I'm not judging here. I hadn't thought about that either until I started writing this book. That's how I ended up on the couch with pizza for my kids and zero energy to function! But really, isn't this where the problem lies? We are doing without thinking. We are going through the motions without being mindful of our intention—the why and how of being a Mom.

So, just what is it we're doing?

JUGGLING TO THE TIPPING POINT

Consider for a moment all the *doing* we actually do on a daily basis. Here is a sample list of the many duties we perform as Moms in a typical 24-hour period:

teacher, healer, nutritionist, cook, safety monitor, time manager, chauffeur, planner, hygienist, mediator, counselor, homemaker, housekeeper, coach, laundress, negotiator, chief tucker-inner, appointment maker, nurturer, errand-runner, financial manager, cheerleader, homework helper, wardrobe consultant, hair stylist, storyteller, repair person . . .

. . . and the list goes on and on. Consistent with the dictionary definitions, we actually do spend a large portion of our time performing various tasks and duties. Combine all of these responsibilities with our additional roles in our families, careers, and communities—email,

Duty first, self second. That's all I've ever known.
—HELEN MIRREN in *The Queen*

relationships, phone calls, volunteer work, projects, events—and any ideas we might have had about what it means to be "Mom" get lost and muddled in the constant juggling of to-do's and responsibilities. Our hectic lifestyle leads us very quickly into the whirlwind of *doing* and we soon become jugglers of the many pieces of our lives.

Now just to clarify, the juggling of tasks and responsibilities, in and of itself, is not really problematic. As women, our brains are actually wired for multitasking. We are very adept at processing and managing several ideas and activities at one time. Have you ever noticed how you can juggle the kids, the shopping list, the office, and the home renovation project all at once, while your husband tends to do one thing at a time . . . when asked?! These are natural differences between men's and women's brains that enable us as Moms to divide our attention and multitask.

But, while juggling is not a problem, juggling multiple pressures and demands all of the time is. Constantly juggling to-do's and responsibilities—both perceived and real—causes all of the external demands in our lives to exceed and outweigh our inner resources for dealing with them. This imbalance between our outer and inner worlds is the tipping point—the critical point at which dramatic consequences begin to occur in our physical, emotional, and spiritual well-being. We run on empty, depleted of our inner resources, disengaged from our maternal instincts and intuition, and disconnected from our sense of who we are and what truly matters to us. Beyond the tipping point, we soon feel like we have nothing left of ourselves to give.

This is NOT what it means to be Mom.

In fact, it is all of these physical, emotional, and spiritual resources and qualities that truly make us "Mom"—our unique talents, personalities, quirks, strengths and passions; our feminine wisdom with its intuition, joy, creativity, and softness; our sense of Self. These are the gifts we have to offer our children, our family, and our communities. Without these inner resources we really are just "doers"—performers of the various tasks and duties of a female parent. Any female can do that. It's not *what* you do, but *how* you do it and what *YOU* bring to the tasks you perform that truly define you as Mom. The key is to recognize, nurture, and use these inner resources so they are at the forefront of your parenting, and everything else you do for that matter.

Enter reinvention . . .

REINVENTION DEFINED

Reinvention is typically thought of as the process of changing something so that it seems different and new—like a makeover where you go somewhere for a few hours, you get a new hairdo, some lipstick, a slick pair of Spanx, and voila! You're a new woman. *Reinventing Mom* is not that kind of change.

Reinvention, for our purposes, comes from a lesser known definition which is *the process of bringing something back into existence.* In this way, *Reinventing Mom* is about bringing back into existence all of the inner resources and qualities that make us uniquely Mom. It is a process that unfolds as we begin to let go of thought patterns and behaviors that no longer serve us and we rediscover all of those deep-seated parts of ourselves we've forgotten. There's no place you have to go and nothing you have to buy for this kind of reinvention. You already have everything you need; you just have to connect with it.

> I believe that one defines oneself by reinvention. To not be like your parents. To not be like your friends. To be yourself. To cut yourself out of stone.
>
> —Henry Rollins

Remember the story of Michelangelo and how he created the statue of David? When asked how he did it, Michelangelo said that in the flawed block of marble he saw an angel, completely shaped and perfect. All he had to do was chisel away everything that wasn't David. In doing that, Michelangelo gave the world a beloved work of art that connects with people in a deep and meaningful way. This is exactly what *Reinventing Mom* is all about.

The Mom and woman you are meant to be is already within you—completely formed and perfect. We just have to chisel away the flawed notions and practices you've acquired over the years from family, friends, our culture, and even yourself, and get rid of everything that is not YOU—all the stuff that keeps us running on empty. As these flawed pieces begin to fall away, you will begin to connect with yourself and the world around you in a much deeper and more joyful way.

So just how do we go about bringing these deep-seated parts of ourselves back into existence? How do we step out of the whirlwind of motherhood to find the purpose and happiness we long for? Just like an artistic endeavor, we begin with the desire to create something beautiful and meaningful. And then we engage in a process.

Unlike most processes in our culture that are outlined step-by-step with a clear beginning and end, reinvention does not have a definitive roadmap or course of development that you can follow. This is a journey that is unique to you and will look and unfold differently for

It is not down in any map; true places never are.

—Herman Melville

each woman who embarks on it. The good news is that there are seven pathways that can guide you and offer you the tools and resources you need along the way . . .

Reinvention as Art

HOW TO THINK LIKE AN ARTIST

Just like reinvention, art is the process of creatively bringing something forth into existence. While you don't have to be Michelangelo to embark on the reinvention journey, thinking like an artist will go a long way in helping you recover the Mom and woman you're meant to be. Here are five principles for thinking with an artist's mind:

- **Curiosity**: a curious approach to life and a willingness to explore and experience new things.
- **Beauty**: finding and appreciating beauty in everyday things.
- **Persistence**: a willingness to learn from mistakes and to keep going, even in the face of hardship.
- **Creativity**: going beyond ordinary ways of thinking and doing things.
- **Faith in the Unknown**: endeavoring something without knowing what exactly the outcome will be.

Having read this far, you are already using the principle of curiosity. Keep reading and you'll be well on your way to an artist's mind.

THE SEVEN PATHWAYS OF REINVENTION

In my own journey of reinvention and my work with fellow Moms, I have found seven key themes or areas that contribute to transforming a running on empty life to a life with more energy, wisdom, purpose, and joy:

Reclaiming your feminine wisdom
Restoring your physical energy and mood
Refocusing emotional and psychological beliefs
Recovering your Self—the YOU that is not "Mom"
Rediscovering a sense of the sacred in your everyday life
Rethinking balance and priorities
Remembering your purpose as a Mom

The pathways focus on all aspects of being: psychological, emotional, physical, and spiritual—everything that makes you who you are as a unique individual. Although the pathways are divided into seven different chapters, it's important to note that all of these areas are closely related and affected by one another. As you begin to focus time and attention on restoring one area, you will support reinvention in the other areas as well.

I would suggest reading through the pathways in order first as many of the ideas are carried through the chapters, and references are made in later pathways to concepts presented earlier. However, when it comes to starting your own journey, it doesn't matter where you begin—the process will be different for everyone. Some women may be drawn to the emotional and psychological pathways of reinvention, feeling emotionally drained in their role as Mom. For others, it might be an overall lack of physical energy and feeling that they can't keep up to the demands of motherhood that brings them to the journey. Still others may begin the process from a spiritual place, feeling a sense of sadness or that something is missing from their lives.

Regardless of where you begin, you will most likely move from one pathway to another over a period of time or work on two or more pathways simultaneously. Most women find that after they've made their way along several pathways over time, they return to earlier pathways they've been on after discovering there is more work to do in those areas. There is no right or wrong way. Whatever feels right to you and seems to work in your unique life is the way to travel on this journey.

I began my own journey of reinvention more than ten years ago when I felt there was something missing in my life. Although I had accomplished much and was successful by most external standards, there was a certain emptiness in my life that I couldn't put my finger on. It

Wherever you are, is exactly where you're supposed to be. Honor that.

—IYANLA VANZANT

was that "existential discomfort" Judith Warner's group of Moms described in her book *Perfect Madness*. It was here that I began my journey along the spiritual path. That work very quickly led me to the emotional and psychological pathways, healing past issues and clearing out ways of thinking that no longer served me. Around that same time, I also began rediscovering who I was as a unique individual and how I could use my gifts and talents in the best interests of my family and my community.

I spent several years on these pathways. It was only after my second child was born in my early- to mid-thirties that I discovered the physical pathway, trying to understand hormonal changes and their effects on mood and energy. (Read: I was trying to find a cure for my constant tiredness and grouchiness!) And as my children got older and life got busier, I revisited my priorities and that very elusive thing called "life balance."

As my journey continues to evolve, I seem to be constantly drawn back to the spiritual pathway, uncovering and connecting with the richness and meaning in my life as a Mom and a woman. This is just how the process has and continues to unfold for me. It's what works in my unique life. Wherever you are in your life as you read this is exactly where you need to be. Begin there. Work through the pathways in whatever way feels right for you. If after reading through the pathways you're unsure about where to begin your journey, start at the first pathway and work your way through the paths as they are laid out. This approach will allow for a natural evolution of reinvention just as well.

WHAT TO PACK

Okay, you're not packing for this journey in the literal sense. But there are a few things you'll want to take with you from a figurative standpoint to make the most of your journey:

❖ *Patience.* Remember that reinvention is a process that unfolds over time. It is not a quick-fix approach to becoming the Mom and woman you are meant to be, so progress and change will not always happen how and when you want it to. Don't rush it. Take your time, be patient and trust in the process.

A journey is like a marriage. The certain way to be wrong is to think you control it.

—JOHN STEINBECK

❖ *Awareness.* Reinventing Mom is about reaching a new level of consciousness in our lives as mothers and women, and tuning in to your inner world of thoughts and feelings is a vital tool for the journey. Most of us have learned to focus on everything outside of ourselves and off into the future as we strive to get things done for our children, our families, and our careers. It's time to shift some of that focus inward and downward and into the present moment so you can do the work of reinvention and connect to your life in a new and meaningful way. You will develop this kind of deep awareness in all areas of your life as you move through the seven pathways. For now, it's helpful to try the "Tuning In" practice below.

❖ *Reflection.* Each of the seven pathways offers questions you can ask yourself, insights you can tell yourself, and reinvention practices that can guide you on your journey. Give yourself the time and space to explore these resources as they are powerful tools for change. You might find it helpful to have a journal or notebook handy to record your thoughts and feelings as you work through the pathways. Using a journal has been a particularly invaluable tool for me on my own journey.

❖ *Action.* An integral part of reinvention is trying out the ideas and information in your daily life. It's one thing to read something and say "Okay, I get that." It's a completely different thing to read something, experience it, and *know* it. Reinventing Mom is about a knowing—a knowing of who you are and how you want to be in the world. And it's about knowing how to be those things for yourself, your partner, and your children. The only way you can truly know these things is to experience them for yourself.

Reinvention Practice

TUNING IN

Many years ago, a yoga instructor introduced me to something called a "walking meditation." The whole purpose of this exercise is to develop inner awareness and present-moment being and it was by far, one of the most profound exercises I've ever tried. Here's what you do:

The next time you're out walking alone somewhere—whether it's at the grocery store, the office, or walking your dog—focus all of your attention in the present moment. Forget about where you're going, what you have to do when you get there, or what you're going to have for dinner. Focus only on what you're doing as you walk.

Be mindful of your breathing. Is it quick and shallow or slow and deep? Feel your legs as they move and your feet as they touch the ground. Notice the swing of your arms. Let go of any tension you feel. Soften your face, your eyes, and your mouth. Relax your shoulders.

After a few minutes, notice any interesting sights, smells, or sounds around you. Take in the pleasure of your surroundings and smile. Remain mindful as you continue to walk and revel in this new found level of awareness.

---

*   *   *   *   *

Humorist Marilyn Grey once said, "We know not where our dreams will take us, but we can probably see quite clearly where we'll go without them." It's time for a new way. You already have everything you need, so . . .

Ready, set, let's reinvent!

Part Two

Seven Pathways of Reinvention

THE RIGHT FRAME OF MIND

Reclaiming the Feminine

So there I was, sitting on the sidelines of the basketball court, cheering and yelling with the other parents for our seven- and eight-year-old girls: "Be more aggressive, honey!" "Get in there! Don't be afraid to get aggressive;" "Gah! I wish she would be more aggressive." Moms and Dads alike are frustrated and bewildered as to why our daughters aren't more determined and forceful.

Amidst all the parental shouting and lamenting, I have one of those surreal moments where you step outside yourself and catch a rare glimpse at what's really going on around you. I see the faces of these young girls and I hear the messages being shouted at them: "be more" and "get aggressive." And in that moment, all I can think to myself is: "What the hell are we doing?"

Fifty years ago, Betty Friedan sparked the feminist revolution with her landmark book, *The Feminine Mystique*, challenging the social and economic notion that a woman's place was in the home. Friedan, like so many others, knew that the potential for women was far greater than the invented life June Cleaver was promising . . . and they set out to prove it.

Since then, women have made amazing and significant strides in society and the workplace. Women have entered the workforce in record numbers. They are obtaining college and university degrees in record numbers. A large percentage of women now hold managerial and executive-level positions and many are leading companies, institutions, and political parties. And for the first time, a growing percentage of mothers are even becoming the primary breadwinners in their families. As Maria Shriver states in her 2009 report *A Woman's Nation*, "Women have now taken their place as powerhouses driving the economy."

We are fortunate to stand on the shoulders of these women today. But as much as women have acquired over the years in gaining this "powerhouse" recognition, it's clear that we have also given up a lot to get here. In breaking through the feminine mystique, women had to disconnect from many of the feminine qualities and biological traits that were highlighted as reasons they belonged in the home—soft, nurturing, emotional, relationship-centered. To prove that they belonged in the then male-dominated workplace, women had to "be more." They had to be strong, assertive, analytical, and high-performing—they had to "get aggressive" in order to compete and succeed. And many did.

Ironically, in spite of all their success and progress, here we are some fifty years later still encouraging our girls to "be more" and "get aggressive." And, even more ironically, while we may be social and economic powerhouses—while we may be strong and confident and ambitious—our girls are overwhelmed and confused by today's cultural pressures and we as Moms and women are still not happier than our own mothers were.

In my own life and my experience with other Moms, I have found that reclaiming the feminine qualities we have inadvertently discounted over the years to be an essential step in reconnecting with who we are as women and mothers. Our feminine wisdom with its intuitive, creative, relational, and emotional qualities is fundamental to who we are; it's part of our nature. Embracing that side of ourselves doesn't mean that we can't also be strong and ambitious. We don't have to don our aprons (if you even have one!) and head back to the kitchen. It simply means we need to understand and embrace all aspects of ourselves if we are to fully become the Moms and women we're meant to be.

> The dilemma for women has often been, 'How do I be those things that are called masculine, like confident and assertive and ambitious, and still be a woman?
>
> —MARIA SHRIVER, *A Woman's Nation*

In order to reclaim our feminine wisdom, it's important to better understand the differences between the feminine/right mind and the masculine/left mind as well as how women's brains are uniquely designed to make use of these differences. Once you have an appreciation for how our unique mind works, we can then look at the many ways to cultivate and care for the feminine qualities we have disconnected from. As you begin to embrace these traits, you will be better able to tune in to the challenges of your everyday life, you will enhance your mental, emotional, and physical health, and you will be laying the foundation for building a rich and meaningful inner life—a reinvented life—in addition to a life of outer success and accomplishment.

RIGHT BRAIN, LEFT BRAIN; GIRL BRAIN, BOY BRAIN

As we know, much of nature is organized in twos: male/female, right/left, yin/yang, rational/intuitive. Our brain is organized in this way as well with a left hemisphere (left brain) and a right hemisphere (right brain). While the left and right brains work together as part of a complementary whole, each side processes information and "sees the world" in uniquely different ways. Let's take a closer look at the differences between the two sides . . .

In many ways, the left brain functions like an assembly line worker. It takes in information in a systematic way and deals with it precisely and orderly—up-down, left-right, first-second-third. It analyzes details, makes comparisons and judgments, then makes decisions according to a set of rules and standards—too messy, too slow, too short, just right. Just like an assembly line, the left brain is always focused on time and what's next. It is highly efficient and an amazing *doer*. Getting everyone up in the morning, dressed, fed, and out the door on time for school and work is a very left brain process.

The language centers of the left brain give our mind the ability to speak to us—sometimes constantly. It's that inner voice, or "brain chatter" that is difficult to turn off and is constantly reminding us about what's on our to-do list, replaying the things we wish we hadn't said or should have said, and complaining about our lack of time to get everything done. And because the left brain tends to work in a rote, repetitive way, we are often unaware of how much chatter actually goes on in there.

Another feature of the left mind is the definition of *self*. Herein lies the center for the ego which provides us with an inner awareness of our identity and everything that makes up our biography. While this is certainly important in remembering who we are and what makes us unique, the ego mind on its own is only concerned with our individuality and our independence. Along with the other features of the left mind, this means critical judgments and comparisons of our self against others. It keeps tabs on and reminds us where we rank according to external standards—the financial scale, parenting scale, attractiveness scale, and every other scale it knows. The notion "be more" resides in this left brain ego center.

> **When I look outside myself and start comparing myself to other people, I weaken a little bit.**
> —Brooke Shields

The right brain is very different in the way it works. Without the rules, standards and time-sensitivity of the left brain, it is free to think creatively and spontaneously without judgment or inhibition. It has a carefree nature that focuses on the "right here, right now," accepting and appreciating people and things exactly as they are in the moment. This present-moment awareness and appreciation is what enables us to experience joy and inner peace and makes the right mind especially gifted at *being*.

In contrast to the step-by-step approach of the left brain, the right mind uses our senses to take in everything all at once and then weaves it together to create a meaningful whole. Moments and issues don't pass by like an assembly line, but are rich with feelings, thoughts, and physiological responses. Think: standing on the beach, the warm sun on your face, the sound of the tide rolling in and out, the warm, soft sand between your toes, the calm relaxation in your body. Ahhhh. This is your right mind at work.

The right mind is also the seat of empathy and compassion. Designed to focus on faces, tone of voice, and body language, our right brain enables us to "read" people and tune in to their feelings and needs—an ability that is especially enhanced in us as mothers. When our children are born, the flood of the hormone oxytocin in our body and brain heightens our senses so that our baby's face, smell, touch, and cry are chemically imprinted on our right brain. This ability enables us to attune to and bond with our children in a very powerful way.

Of course, a discussion of the right mind would not be complete without mentioning intuition—the gift of sensing or knowing something through feeling versus fact. The ability to take in information through our senses and make meaningful connections or "leaps of insight" without figuring everything out is a large part of our intuitive genius. It's how we can look at our toddler and sense he is coming down with a cold long before the first sniffle or cough appears or greet our teenager and feel her distress from a bad day. The nudges and gut feelings we get from our intuition provide valuable insight and knowledge to guide us.

And, where the left mind houses our ego awareness and definition of *self*, the right mind is home to our essence awareness and concept of *Self*. Our essence is not concerned with our biography and the details about what we do. It is concerned with the deeper parts of who we are—the parts of ourselves that are unchanging and make us a unique human being. It reminds us what makes us laugh and cry, what brings us joy, what we love and what we long for. Along with the other features of the right mind, our essence awareness connects us to the bigger picture. It values our relationships with others, embraces our *inter*dependence, and enables us to experience a connection with something greater than ourselves.

The Left and the Right of It

COMPARING THE LEFT AND RIGHT MINDS

L mind		**R** mind	
Rational	*Draws conclusions based on reason and fact*	Intuitive	*Draws conclusions based on hunches, feelings or images*
Linear	*Looks at the parts, one after the other, and links ideas together*	Holistic	*Sees the whole picture— overall patterns and relationships*
Sequential	*Does things in an orderly fashion—first, second, third, etc.*	Simultaneous	*Deals with multiple ideas and items at once*

Independent	*Focuses on self-sufficiency*	Relational	*Relationship-centered*
Factual	*Concerned with facts and the bottom line*	Emotional	*Concerned with feelings and meaning*
Ego-aware	*Concerned with identity of self based on external standards*	Essence-aware	*Connected to deeper parts of Self based on inner feelings*
Judgmental	*Critically examines and disapproves*	Appreciative	*Embraces and accepts gratefully*
Focused	*Remains fixed on the end goal*	Relaxed	*Revels in the present moment*
Practical	*Thinks sensibly and focuses on what is realistic*	Imaginative	*Thinks creatively and focuses on what is possible*

Can you see where your mind tends to reside in much of your daily life? Chances are, like the majority of Moms in our culture, you spend your time in a routine checking things off your to-do list, striving to get things done, with constant mind chatter reminding you how little time there is and what's next. You live in your left mind with little or no time for present moment being. While you may be thinking, "That's how everybody functions in today's world," the truth is that this left mind way of living actually goes against our very nature as women. Our feminine brain is uniquely designed for maximizing the use of both the right and left brains as well as for using the many gifts of the right mind.

As Michael Gurian writes in his bestselling book, *The Wonder of Girls*, "Let's go deep into the female mind, and let this be a doorway into wonderful mysteries . . ."

How Our Feminine Mind Works

Thanks to the work of neuroscientists such as Louann Brizendine (*The Female Brain*) and Mona Lisa Schulz (*The New Feminine Brain*) it's become clear that women have a unique brain. Contrary to what pioneering feminists believed, our brain *is* different from a man's brain—it is wired differently, it has its own ways of thinking, feeling, and seeing the world, and it has unique gifts and abilities, especially in the areas of emotion, connection, and intuition. (It also has its own set of challenges such as those with mood, depression, and anxiety which we will explore in Path Two.) We come into the world with our unique wiring already in place and through the various stages of our lives, our female brain develops quite differently from our male counterparts. Here are some of the key differences as described by Brizendine and Schulz:

- Overall, the female brain has a lot more connections—between the left and right brains and between different brain areas. The bundle of fibers connecting the left and right brains (the *corpus callosum*) is twenty-five percent larger in women, enabling much more cross talk between our left and right minds. This greater connectivity is what enables us to more aptly talk about feelings, use our intuition, and juggle multiple things at one time. With fewer connections, the male brain tends to be more "compartmentalized" to the left mind.

- Communication and emotion centers are larger in our female brain as is the capacity to read other people—their feelings, needs, and state of mind. These differences make us uniquely wired for the right brain aptitudes of emotional sensitivity, empathy, and forming deep connections with others. When you need a shoulder to cry on or a listening ear, men, women, and children alike turn to women, especially to Mom.

> **Women have a superhighway going on in there. Men have this little corked country road, and you're lucky if a word gets over.**
> —ROBERT BLY

- The feminine mind is more sensitive to body awareness and the bodily sensations processed in the right brain. According to Schulz, this hyperconnectivity between the right brain and body is referred to as the *mind-body intuition network*. This network enhances our intuition and inner guidance, especially when it comes to our health and well-being and the well-being of our family. The more compartmentalized male brain tends to shut out this kind of body-brain information.

- The estrogen-dominant female brain (estrogen being the "intimacy" hormone) steers us towards the right brain traits of intimate connection, social harmony, and cohesiveness—skills that are essential to bonding with our children and maintaining a cohesive family unit. The testosterone-dominant male brain, on the other hand, tends to direct men towards the left brain traits of independence and competition.

It's clear that our biology has hardwired us to make special use of the right mind traits of emotional awareness, intuition and inner guidance, and the ability to connect deeply with others. Our increased connectivity also gives us greater access to the many other gifts the right mind has to offer—creativity, joy, meaning, and an inner sense of Self. These right mind traits along with our unique wiring for drawing on them is what comprises our feminine wisdom—a truly remarkable gift.

So how is it that we have disconnected from such tremendous aptitudes that are hardwired into our brain?

THE FEMININE DISCONNECT

Over the last fifty years as women have strived to fit into a male-dominated workplace, our brain has had to over-develop left mind, masculine traits to adapt and succeed—compartmentalizing emotion and empathy to make key business decisions, focusing on rationale and fact to provide tangible proof, and working to meet deadlines in order to produce results. Our school system also focuses primarily on a left brain thinking style, so children begin developing logical, goal-oriented thought at a very young age. This left brain approach has even filtered into family life where families now hold "family conferences," play dates are organized and scheduled—complete with mommy/child business cards, and our daughters are encouraged to "get in there and be aggressive." Over time, the left brain, masculine style we've adopted and strengthened has muted the feminine wisdom our unique wiring affords us.

I first became aware of my own left brain lopsidedness when I was a graduate student. I had entered a Neuropsychology program with a background in Dance (the subject of another book!) and had worked extremely hard to prove my worthiness of being there. I was successful by most external standards: I had completed a lot of research, published and presented papers, and even won a scholarship. I was an accomplished doer. But the day my research supervisor acknowledged me and a colleague of mine by saying, "Thank you for all the hard work you've done. You girls are machines!" my right mind intuition could no longer be silenced. It faintly whispered that maybe there was something more than producing like a machine.

It took a long time for me to begin trusting that inner voice. My logical left mind was strongly developed from years of schooling and being exposed to messages of success and empowerment in the media. It told me I didn't have time to deal with messy feelings if I wanted to be successful. It said I was foolish to consider anything other than what I already had invested so much in. It warned me what other people would say if I were to change my mind. It tried to convince me to keep going, that I should put on a happy face and the feelings would pass. And it dangled the rewards I stood to lose if I gave in to my "woo-woo" inner voice. The left mind can be relentless in its need to maintain control. It will rationalize, judge, ruminate, justify, shame, and distract to help us achieve outer success. Of course, my right mind knew differently and I eventually, and gradually, allowed it to guide me. (More about following this inner guidance is in Path Four.)

Testosterone: Not Just for Men

THE EFFECTS OF TESTOSTERONE ON MOTHERHOOD

Testosterone is a sex hormone that promotes initiative and motivation for achieving goals in the outer world. It allows for focused, assertive, unemotional thinking and behavior and is produced in relatively high quantities in men. But women produce testosterone, too. And the amount we produce is affected by a number of factors including our menstrual cycle, stress, and social pressures.

Recent research has shown that as women's ambition and social status increase, so does her level of testosterone. This is not surprising given her need to compete and thrive in the workplace, but becomes especially problematic for the right brain, estrogen-based demands of motherhood.

Many women who trade in their high-testosterone careers for the estrogen-soaked vocation of stay-at-home motherhood experience a "culture shock" and are at greater risk for depression and other mood disorders. Others who try to balance their ambitious careers with the demands of motherhood find it difficult to shift gears at the end of the day—from high-powered professional to nurturing caretaker.

Restoring the estrogen-rich right brain and being able to integrate it with the testosterone-laden left brain is key to reconciling this dilemma.

Source: Schulz, M.L. (2005). The New Feminine Brain. *New York: Free Press.*

The fact is that today's social and economic pressures continue to force us to stay in our left brain, creating a separation between our outer world of goals and responsibilities and our inner world of feelings and desires. This disconnect becomes especially problematic for us as Moms. With our inborn feminine wiring underneath our masculine thinking styles, we struggle to find a balance between the left brain initiative and motivation of personal ambition and a successful career with the right brain nurturance and intimacy of motherhood and family. When we're at work, we worry about our children in someone else's care and we feel like we should be home with them. And when we're at home, we have difficulty sitting and just being with our children, worrying about deadlines and all the to-dos we have to

> **Today in our fast-paced, logical, linear, outer-oriented world, it is all too easy for us to forget our female story.**
> —GAIL STRAUB

accomplish. This divide is one of the biggest challenges we face as mothers. And unless we learn to recognize and embrace our right mind, feminine traits in our everyday lives, we set ourselves up for emotional, spiritual, and physical problems.

The Mommy Diaries

I CAN'T SIT STILL!

I envy other mothers who can just sit and play with their kids. I can't do it. Maybe because I'm a go-getter and I've been working in this business since I was eighteen I'm wired a little differently than other women. I just don't have the patience to sit and play Barbies or watch Barney on TV. My mind is constantly thinking about all the things I should be doing, whose call I have to return, what emails I need to send, and how I'm going to solve problems that come up.

I see some of my mom friends sitting with their kids, reading stories, and hanging out. I don't know how they do it! I wish I could sit still long enough and just relax with my kids, but I don't think things would ever get done if I did that. I certainly wouldn't be able to do what I do now.

Lisa, Mom of two, media personality and entrepreneur

In her groundbreaking book, *The New Feminine Brain*, neuropsychiatrist and intuitive expert Mona Lisa Schulz points out the dangers of trapping ourselves in the comfort of our left brain's tidy, efficient, ordered environment: "If your right brain's emotions and intuition don't have equal input into decisions and actions, they initiate biochemical and hormonal events that trigger physical and emotional problems: chronic depression, anxiety, panic, dementia, heart disease, immune system dysfunction, and cancer are the products of an overly dominant left brain, a silenced right brain, and censored intuition."

We can no longer ignore our biology. As our society becomes more complex and we continue to contend with our many roles as Moms—to be caregivers, manage careers, run households, connect with our partners, and

> **If in the name of free will— and political correctness— we try to deny the influence of biology on the brain, we begin fighting our own nature.**
>
> —LOUANN BRIZENDINE, *The Female Brain*

be active in our communities—we must learn to respect and embrace our right mind feminine wisdom. Reclaiming these qualities may seem uncomfortable because it goes against politically correct conventions of female ambition and self-sufficiency or because talk of feelings and intuition may seem "woo-woo." But this wisdom is hardwired into us and for us to focus primarily on doing and striving in the name of social and economic independence is to deny a major aspect of being a Mom and woman.

As we begin to explore some of the ways we can restore our feminine wisdom, I hope you will come to see that part of being the Moms and women we're meant to be lies in fully embracing our right brain feminine qualities as well as finding a balance between our left mind/outer world and our right mind/inner world.

MAKING THE RIGHT SHIFT

At just thirty-seven years of age, Harvard-trained brain scientist Jill Bolte Taylor suffered a massive stroke in the left side of her brain. For a period of time her left brain did not function and she experienced a rare glimpse into the reality of the intuitive, feeling-centered, all-encompassing right brain. In her bestselling book, *My Stroke of Insight*, Jill recounts her incredible story, describing her right brain reality as a state of complete inner peace and well-being. This priceless gift, she says, led her to recalibrate her view of the world and to recognize that peace and well-being are never more than a thought away. We only need to "step to the right" of our left brain and its incessant chatter to find it.

This section will help you learn how to "step to the right." We'll explore intuition (what it is and how you can tune in to it), emotional awareness and connection, as well as creativity. The more you understand and become aware of these right mind traits—what they feel like and how to use them—the more you will restore and embrace your feminine wisdom. Let's take a walk on the right side . . .

Nudges, Gut Feels, and Vibes: Awakening Your Intuition

When I first started putting this program together for Moms, I wasn't sure what to call it. I had considered several titles, but none really seemed to capture the essence of what I was trying to convey. And they certainly weren't unique or engaging. Until one day, I was sitting alone in my office jotting down some ideas for the overview of the program when the term "Reinventing Mom" flashed in my mind. As quickly as the words had appeared, I knew that was the title.

This is intuition. It's a flash of insight that is not mediated by any analysis or rational thought—it just comes to us. And it doesn't always come as a big "aha" breakthrough or a fanfare of epiphany. Intuition tends to be subtle and quiet. It more often comes as a whisper, a gentle nudge, or a persistent feeling or thought. This is why it often gets drowned out by the louder, more dominant chatter of our left mind.

Depending on your unique personality, intuition can come through in a number of different ways. It can come through emotions as an inner feeling of sadness, doubt, or calmness. For some, it surfaces in the body as fatigue, illness, uneasiness in the stomach, or other body sensations. Others receive intuitive information primarily through images, ideas, songs, and dreams. And some feel most in touch with their intuition through spiritual or religious practices such as prayer and meditation. Getting in touch with how your intuition comes through for you will help you recognize and make sense of your own intuitive insights.

Here are three ways you can begin to get in touch with your intuition:

1. *Quiet the mind.* This is a real challenge for many. We're so accustomed to the constant chatter in our minds that the noise has become a natural presence in our lives. How often do you go to bed with a stream of chatter going through your head—tomorrow's to-dos, today's incompletes, unresolved issues, worries, and disappointments—unable to turn it off? This is a common experience for many of the Moms I work with. We've forgotten what silence is like. Many even find silence uncomfortable.

   > The secret to seeing—really seeing—is quieting the bossy know-it-all left brain so the mellower right brain can do its magic.
   >
   > —DANIEL PINK, A WHOLE NEW MIND

   If the idea of silence scares the bejeebers out of you, don't worry. I'm not going to suggest you sit in solitary confinement with a robe and burning incense. Quieting the mind is a lot less daunting and can be as simple as finding a few minutes alone in quiet space to relax and let your left brain unwind: taking a quiet walk in nature, soaking in a warm bubble bath, enjoying a cup of tea on the porch, or simply curling up with a blanket in your favorite chair. The goal here is just to let your left mind chatter go. Step to the right and just *be* in those few moments.

   Of course, your left mind won't give up that easily. It will flit around from one thought to another, reminding you of anything and everything. Buddhists call this "monkey mind." But as the thoughts come up, simply let them go. Step to the right and just be there. Notice your surroundings—don't judge, just notice. Relax your body. Take a few deep breaths and let out a few big sighs. Step to the right and quiet your mind. This practice is the beginning of present-moment being and will give your intuition the opportunity to come through.

2. *Be in your body.* As you read earlier, the body is a rich source of intuitive information through the right brain's mind-body network. Being aware of our body's sensations and feelings opens us up to intuitive messages about our health and well-being. Running on empty symptoms such as fatigue, feeling "off-center," disconnected, or drained are part of the body's internal messaging system. They let us know that it's time to slow down, refuel, and reconnect to life. Attuning to these inner signals and heeding their call is essential not only for stepping to the right, but also for the reinvention journey.

Unfortunately, we spend most of our time stuck in our heads and are rarely in tune with what's going on in our bodies. In many ways, we are like great big heads walking around— all of our focus is stuck up in our heads! In Path Two we will explore in much more depth "being in the body" as part of restoring your physical energy. For now, a great place to start this reconnection is through sensual experiences: massage, pedicures, bubble baths, aromatherapy, sexual intimacy, yoga, dance. The "Tuning In" walking meditation described in the previous chapter is also a great practice for being in your body.

As you engage in these activities, let your focus shift down into your body and pay attention to how it feels. Notice any tension. Do you sense physical discomfort, achiness, or numbness anywhere? A knot in your stomach? A lump in your throat? Is your mind swirling with information and noise? Are there areas that are at ease and relaxed? Does your body's energy feel vibrant and energized or dull and depleted? The more intimately you know your body and can be in your body, the more successful you will be in noticing and receiving its intuitive messages and feminine wisdom.

3. *Tune in to your intuitive language.* As you learn to quiet your mind and be in your body, you can start to pay attention to your intuition and how it comes through for you. Here are some of the more common ways intuition speaks:

- An inner sense or gut feeling that something is not right or that everything is okay. For example, feeling that your child is not well despite what your pediatrician has told you or sensing that a relationship will mend in spite of a dispute or break-up.
- Ideas, images, or symbols flash in your mind—like how I got the idea for the title *Reinventing Mom.*
- Vivid, highly memorable dreams. I once had a vivid dream about a duck in a red raincoat, rubber boots, and rain hat. A

The mind can assert anything and believe it has proved it. My beliefs I test on my body, on my intuitional consciousness, and when I get a response there, then I accept it.

—D.H. LAWRENCE

dream dictionary rightly explained that I was shielding myself from emotions related to following my passion.

- A *knowing* about something yet to happen—contact from a certain person, that your name is to be called, an upcoming pregnancy.
- Songs, quotes, or words play in your head. A fellow Mom I know had been worried for months about how to help her troubled teen, when one day the Beatles' song *Let It Be* played in her head and she knew things would work out in their own time.
- An inner voice offers guidance, encouragement, or direction. At first it may be difficult to know if this is your intuition "coming through" or your imagination "making it up." My rule of thumb is: if it feels right, go with it. Chances are the information is relevant either way.
- Body sensations such as tingling, shivers up the spine, a knot in the stomach, or feeling physically drained—each offers intuitive guidance about staying on track, following your gut, or slowing down.

Remember that intuition is a very natural ability—most of us have just disconnected from it. With awareness and practice, you can reconnect with this gift quite readily. If you are keeping a journal, jot down any intuitive messages you notice. This practice will enhance your awareness and appreciation of your intuition and how it comes through for you. In time, intuitive feelings will become second nature and you will be able to notice and follow these pieces of feminine wisdom much more effortlessly.

Reinvention Practice

SIGNS AND SYNCHRONICITIES

Because intuition allows us to take in information and make meaningful connections without logical analysis, part of its genius lies in seeing signs and synchronicities. Synchronicities are coincidences or "divine nudges" that occur when inner thoughts and outer events come together in a way that is meaningful, yet can't be explained. Here are some examples:

- ❖ You are thinking about taking a course then suddenly receive a flyer in the mail with information on how to register.
- ❖ You are struggling with a parenting issue then stumble across an article with advice on how to solve the problem.

As you strengthen and appreciate your intuition, you will begin to notice these kinds of signs and synchronicities happening in your own life. I think of them as special nudges that help support and guide our innermost thoughts and feelings.

Here are some ways you can tap into and work with synchronicity:

❖ Pay close attention to meaningful coincidences that happen to you. The more you notice and embrace them, the more they will show up.

❖ Notice names or unusual phrases that keep showing up, when something you need ironically appears, or when you receive an act of kindness at just the right time.

❖ Write about these coincidences—large or small—in a journal and consider what the messages are for you.

Up Close and Personal: Tuning In to Feeling and Connection

Some time ago, I received one of those "tell-about-yourself" emails that was circulating amongst a group of fellow Moms. There's a series of questions, you answer each, and then forward the email on so others can learn about you. By the time I received it, dozens of Moms had already answered the questions and I was very saddened to learn that the vast majority of them couldn't remember the last time they had cried. When was the last time you cried?

Now, truth be told, I'm a bit of a weeper. I cry at touching moments on TV, when people open meaningful gifts, and when my children say or do heartfelt things. And depending on the time of month, I have even been known to cry at Christina Aguilera ballads on the radio. (Sad, I know, yet still true.) I certainly don't believe that everyone needs to be this emotional, but hearing that so many women couldn't remember the last time they cried reminded me how our shift to the left over the years has hardened us in many ways. We have learned to hide and deny our feelings—the soft, feminine parts of our being—in order to function in today's world. It's no wonder we have a hard time feeling joy.

> **Woman has learned to ignore her own feeling needs . . . as she pushes ahead in a pressure-filled, production-oriented life.**
>
> —JUDITH DUERK, *Circle of Stones*

Stepping to the right and reclaiming our feminine wisdom involves a softening, a shift from the head to the heart. We must allow ourselves to really feel again—to open up to the full range of our emotions and listen to them rather than stuff them away and put on a happy face so we can forge ahead with our to-do lists. While choosing the rational over the emotional may seem practical, enabling us to remain in control and productive, it is certainly not joyful or meaningful. When we allow ourselves to connect with feeling we open up to the world in a new way, deepening our relationship with our Self, the people around us, and life itself.

Tuning in to feeling simply involves noticing and accepting. Here's how to begin: Over the next day or two, start paying attention to the various feelings you experience and write about them in a journal or notebook. What do you notice? If you tend to reside in your rational left mind much of the time, you might notice a lot of feelings related to thoughts about efficiency, time, and meeting expectations—frustration, impatience, guilt, anger, resentment, worry, fear, or stress. How often do you feel happy, calm, patient, forgiving, loving, or compassionate? Were you inspired or moved—either to tears or laughter, or even just to feel *something*? Did you miss opportunities to experience these feel-good emotions?

Whatever emotions come up, don't censor them, dismiss them as unimportant, or reason them away. Just notice them and write about whatever you are feeling. Remember that if you discount your own feelings, you are also likely to discount the feelings of others, including those of your children and partner. I've often heard parents tell their children "Don't be silly. You shouldn't feel that way." Or "Stop crying. We don't have time for this." All feelings matter and are acceptable—it's how you deal with those feelings that makes the difference. We'll learn a lot more about dealing with emotions in Path Three. For now, just focus on noticing and accepting.

If your left mind is particularly skilled at denying emotions, you might have a difficult time noticing any feeling at all. That's okay. Keep paying attention and writing about what comes up— you're frustrated with your kids' bickering, worried about the piles of laundry, happy about your new handbag, feeling guilty over eating a carton of Haagen-Dazs. It's all good. Just accept the feelings and write about them. Eventually you will learn to move past the rational left mind and connect with a lot of the rich feeling and wisdom that has been buried away in your feminine right mind. With time and practice, you'll be amazed at what you discover there.

Now, be prepared. Your left mind is going to fight you on this "woo-woo" writing exercise. It will say all the same things it says to feeling, "I don't have time for this," "This is not important," "I won't really benefit from this." Thank your left mind for its opinion and do the writing anyway. Carve out some quiet time and space in your schedule and write the right stuff (right mind, not right correct!). I find writing before bed the best time to reflect and get out all of my feelings and experiences from the day. Other women swear by doing this kind of writing first thing in the morning to clear their head and connect with their feminine side before the day begins. Depending on the age of your children, you might schedule this time during their naptime or when you take some time for yourself. (If time to yourself sounds like a foreign concept, don't worry. We'll be dealing with this issue in more detail in Path Four.)

Q: Why do we write in a journal?

A: To get to the other side.

—JULIA CAMERON, *The Artist's Way*

If you feel stuck on what to write, here are some sentence stems to help you get started:

- Today, I felt . . .
- I am worried about . . .
- I feel most happy when . . .
- My left brain chatter is telling me . . .
- I am angry that . . .
- I am grateful for . . .

As you become more in tune with feeling and begin to connect with your inner Self, you will also develop a kind of "feeling antenna." This feeler will not only give you clearer reception of your own feelings and allow you to "change the frequency" if you choose, but will also enable you to be more in tune with the people around you and how they feel. You will be more sensitive and compassionate about feeling and more inclined to see the world through "soft eyes." In fact, in her book about having a left brain stroke, Jill Bolte Taylor describes the visual system of the right mind as actually seeing the world in a "blended or softened" way, enabling us to focus on the bigger picture of how things connect with one another. This softening and connection with our Self and others is a deeply feminine way of being and is how we begin to rediscover love and joy in our lives. It's how we begin to reconnect to the Moms and women we're meant to be.

Real Play: Getting Creative and Having Fun

When we spend our time in left mind ways of thinking and doing, we tend to take life way too seriously, focusing on getting things done and seeing results. Everything begins to feel like a chore and we forget what it's like to be inspired and enjoy life. Stepping to the right and embracing creativity, imagination, and play is a wonderful antidote to the rote and stuffy left way of living. And because we are creative beings by nature as women, engaging in creative pursuits allows us to express ourselves in new ways and to experience a lightheartedness and joyfulness we are often missing.

Okay, so what shall we do?!

There is virtually no shortage of ways we can get creative and have fun. To start, just watch your children. Before the age of about six or seven, our kids have wonderful imaginations and really know how to play—simply for the sake of having fun. Like me, you've no doubt spent countless hours being pulled in to dress-up sessions, play-dough making, superhero battles, and

Real play is . . . a ridiculous, imaginative, creative way of looking at life and entering into it magically—upside down, sideways or backwards.

—Laura Corn

singing and dancing to Barney (yes, that big purple dinosaur is still around!). These are very easy ways to step away from our left minds for a while and use our imaginations.

Of course, after the twentieth time you've sung the same Barney song or eaten more play-dough cookies than you can count, you might be feeling the need for a more "grown-up" creative pursuit. In this case, any artistic endeavor will enable you to tap into your right frame of mind: painting, gardening, woodworking, knitting, decorating, cooking, writing, scrapbooking, photography, music, or sewing to name a few. You might sign up for a class you've always wanted to take or create a space in your home to develop a passion you've been putting off. Even the process of journaling can be a great creative endeavor. What is essential to this process, is finding something that resonates with you and that you'll enjoy doing.

Creative pursuits do not have to be grandiose projects that result in magnificent masterpieces. Unless you are looking to turn your creativity into your work, "creative dabbling" might be the way to go here. For example, I took a knitting class several years ago and in the process managed to knit a baby blanket for my niece. Since then, though, I've started knitting scarves, blankets, and throws never to finish any of them. While my left brain says, "Tsk, tsk. All that wasted time and money," my right mind is quite content to just dabble in knitting when the spirit strikes. I also enjoy gardening and decorating and love looking through home and garden magazines at the beautiful, creative ideas inside. Do I have amazing gardens and a picture perfect home? No, but I love to dabble in the creative process. What's great about creative dabbling is that it allows you to just focus on the process. There are no timelines or deadlines and you don't have to worry about the end-result—you simply create for the pure pleasure and right-mindedness of it.

Journalist and author Brenda Ueland once responded to the question: *Why should we all use our creative power?* by saying, "Because there is nothing that makes people so generous, joyful, lively, bold and compassionate, so indifferent to fighting and the accumulation of objects and money." Count me in.

Reinvention Practice

THE ART OF GALUMPHING

Anthropologists have found "galumphing" to be one of the essential talents that characterize higher animals and people. It is the happy, creative playfulness we see in puppies, kittens, children, and baby chimpanzees, as well as in young groups and communities. To galumph is to hop instead of walk, to eat ice cream and make a mess, and to dance like no one is watching. Galumphing is of considerable evolutionary value as it is what allows us to counter the vast amounts of information we take in. In other words, we need to galumph in order to de-stress and shift from left to right.

Take some time this week to galumph. If you've got little ones at home, you can simply join in their galumphing—sing and dance to some fun music, build a blanket fort, dress up, have a tea party, swing as high as you can on a swing set, go for a walk and collect cool rocks. If your children are older, you can recruit them to galumph with you—have a water balloon fight in your yard, play a game of Twister, go to a funny movie and laugh. The possibilities are endless.

Yes, your left mind is probably balking at galumphing in a big way. Tell it not to be such a stick-in-the-mud and do it anyway.

Source: Nachmanovitch, S. (1990). Free Play: The Power of Improvisation in Life and the Arts, *New York: Jeremy P. Tarcher/Perigree Books.*

STAYING RIGHT TO GO LEFT

Making the right shift doesn't mean we discount our left mind intelligence and rational thought. It means we are aware enough and connected enough to our right mind wisdom that we are no longer slave to our left brain. Remember that the left and right minds are designed to work together as a smooth, integrated whole. The left mind on its own can be a tyrannical ruler, while the right mind on its own would be like living in La La Land. As we become more skilled at tuning in to and using our feminine wisdom, we develop versatile minds that can

> **Motherly love is not much use if it expresses itself only as a warm gush of emotion, delicately tinged with pink. It must also be strong, guiding and unselfish.**
>
> —RACHEL BILLINGTON

effectively integrate all of the gifts our right and left minds have to offer. We'll no longer feel the need to compete and "get aggressive" in order to follow our ambitions. We will be soft, yet still strong and confident. We will be intuitive, compassionate, and creative while still getting things done . . . and feel more joy and connection while doing it.

* * * * *

In his bestselling book, *A Whole New Mind: Why Right-Brainers Will Rule the Future*, Daniel Pink points out that the age of left brain dominance is coming to an end and that the future belongs to creative, empathic right brain thinkers. This is the future our children are headed towards and the future we have been uniquely designed for. As mothers and women, I believe that we are the pioneers to lead the way. Reclaiming our innate feminine wisdom is a step in that right direction.

The Mommy Diaries

CHANGING HATS

I always found it hard to come home from work at the end of the day and shift from working woman role to the mom-at-home role. As soon as I walked through the front door, my kids would be all over me asking me for help with something or telling me about another thing. I just felt bombarded and overwhelmed and then that feeling would stick with me for the rest of the day. Finally, I got the idea to ask my kids for ten free minutes when I come home to "change my hat." Now when I walk through the front door we all say hello and hug, but no one bombards me with requests and information. I go upstairs to my room and change my clothes which allows me to make the shift from worker to mother. It's a small thing, but it changes my whole state of mind and allows me to get through the rest of the day a little calmer and happier.

Kathleen, Mom of two and hospital administrator

REFLECTION AND ACTION FOR PATH ONE

❋ Go to your local bookstore or gift shop and treat yourself to a beautiful journal—something that inspires you and that you'll love to write your innermost thoughts and feelings in.

❋ Consider how left—or right-brain dominant you are. Do you spend a lot of time in your left mind? Do you get stuck there, obsessing about time and getting things done; comparing yourself to other Moms; worrying about getting everything "just right"? Try to catch yourself getting stuck in your left mind, then shift to the right. Shift your attention to the present moment and soften. How easy or difficult it is for you to make this shift?

❋ Which part(s) of your feminine wisdom do you feel most disconnected from? Which one(s) do you feel most connected to? Creativity, intuition, emotional connection? Consider how these feminine strengths and disconnects will affect what your children learn. What steps can you take to reconnect with those parts of your feminine wisdom?

FURTHER READING FOR PATH ONE

Returning to My Mother's House: Taking Back the Wisdom of the Feminine by Gail Straub. (New York: High Point, 2008)

A beautiful, heartfelt story filled with insight and wisdom on how to build and sustain an inner life—our feminine wisdom—in a fast-paced world.

My Stroke of Insight: A Brain Scientist's Personal Journey by Jill Bolte Taylor, Ph.D. (New York: Viking, 2008)

A Harvard-trained neuroscientist recounts her story of suffering a left brain stroke and her profound discovery of right- and left-mind realities.

The Female Brain by Louann Brizendine, M.D., Ph.D. (New York: Free Press, 2005)

For those looking for a more scientific understanding of the female brain, Dr. Brizendine's bestselling book is a great resource touching on all aspects of a woman's life—from girlhood to motherhood and beyond.

Developing Intuition: Practical Guidance for Daily Life by Shakti Gawain. (Novato: New World Publishing, 2000)

This bestselling classic guides readers into developing their intuition and allowing it to become a guiding force in their lives.

The Artist's Way, Tenth Anniversary Edition by Julia Cameron. (New York: Tarcher, 2002)

An international bestseller on the subject of creativity and an invaluable guide to helping readers cultivate their creative selves.

Wild Succulent Woman by SARK. (New York: Fireside, 1997)

Author, artist, and acclaimed teacher on the subject of creativity, SARK (Susan Ariel Rainbow Kennedy) explores topics such as love, romance, money, fear, and creativity, inviting women to live a rich and inspired life.

PATH 2

FEMALE FIZZIOLOGY

Restoring Your Physical Energy and Mood

Dear Kelly,

I am thirty-four years old and the mother of two boys, five and two. I have been working from home part time for over a year now. My husband works outside the home, but it's nothing too time constraining. Lately I have been feeling extremely exhausted. I do the bare minimum around the house and find myself wanting to just lay on the couch and watch TV rather than do anything. I would love for our house to be more organized, but I'm not even sure where to start, so I don't ever begin. I have been fighting with my husband more than usual and have been very short tempered with my children. I feel like I am failing as a mom and just can't keep going this way. Any suggestions or advice would be helpful!

My inbox and seminars are filled with Moms just like this. They're tired, grouchy, and unhappy. They feel guilty about not being the Moms and women they want to be. They want to enjoy motherhood and their lives, but can't and have no idea why. Having been there myself, I know exactly why. They are physically running on empty.

Most of the low energy, moodiness, and even weight gain and low sex drive, we experience as Moms is related to lifestyle. We spend our time being on-demand and on-the-go, looking after everyone else's needs to the point that our own basic physiological needs get ignored: we eat poorly—skipping meals and grabbing whatever we can to go; we become sleep deprived and rely on caffeine and sugar "pick-me-ups" to get us through the day; we lack exercise, sunlight, and fresh air; and we spend more time face-to-face with computers and smartphones than we do with our loved ones. It's no wonder we feel less than human!

This lifestyle—this "way"—that we're living goes against our very nature. While civilization has evolved by leaps and bounds over the centuries, the human body has not. Biologically, we still have the same needs that our cavewoman predecessors would have had during the Stone Age. But with the onset of our modern day conveniences such as motorized vehicles, processed food, television, and computer devices, we have fallen out of tune and out of touch with our body's natural rhythms. And when this rhythm falls out of sync, our bodies and brains go haywire and we begin to fizzle out.

OUR NATURAL RHYTHMS: A "HORMONIC" SYMPHONY

As women, the natural rhythms of our bodies are largely dependent on hormones. Hormones are the chemical messengers that travel through our body and brain directing everything our cells do to manage energy, mood, sleep, sex drive, motivation, and hunger. All of our hormones interact and work together in a finely orchestrated symphony, so when you understand how they fall out of sync, you'll understand how we fall out of sync.

Researchers have identified over 200 different types of hormones, but for our purposes we only need to focus on a few key ones: sex hormones (estrogen, progesterone, testosterone), metabolic hormones (insulin, thyroid), and stress hormones (cortisol, adrenaline). For women, the sex hormones are by far the most influential. These hormones shift dramatically every month (as we all know!) and create a delicate balance with every other hormone in our body. In this way, estrogen, progesterone, and testosterone are like the maestros of our inner hormonic symphony.

In his book, *Dr. Robert Greene's Perfect Balance*, Dr. Greene offers the helpful image of a mobile (yes, the same kind you would hang over a baby's crib) to describe women's intricately balanced hormonal system: "Just as every part of a mobile is interconnected and shifts when one section moves, each of your hormones is interrelated to the others, and a shift in the level of one will invariably affect the level of another, as well as the overall balance of your system." Not surprisingly, sex hormones are at the very center of our "personal hormonal mobiles" according to Dr. Greene, because they play the central role in our hormone balance.

When our hormonal mobile is balanced and there's a natural rhythm flowing within our body and brain, we feel good. We're happy, vibrant, energetic, and focused. When the mobile balance goes askew—when there is too much of one hormone or not enough of another—things fall out of sync, communication between our body and brain gets distorted, and we feel moody, sluggish, unmotivated, and even flat out frumpy as a result.

Q: Our baby was born last week. When will my wife begin to feel and act normal again?

A: When the kids are in college.

—ANONYMOUS

Of course, some of the imbalances that occur in this symphony of hormones are a result of natural fluctuations in our monthly cycles and at various life stages (I'm sure you remember all too well the hormonal swings that led to "baby brain" during pregnancy). But because these are natural variations, a healthy hormonal system will restore balance all on its own. The irregular imbalances that lead to the running on empty symptoms many Moms experience are most always a result of our modern lifestyle choices—our eating habits, exercise routines (or lack thereof), and the hectic, stressful pace of our lives. These habits are the breezes and gusts of wind that affect our personal hormonal mobiles on a daily basis. Hormonal imbalances due to lifestyle occur over time and gradually become a way of living for us, often to the point where we don't even realize it's happening. That's when life starts to feel like one big PMS fest. In these cases, lifestyle adjustments are needed in order to restore harmony and balance to our hormones and our lives.

Our Life in Hormones

HOW FEMALE HORMONES AFFECT ENERGY, MOOD, AND INTUITION

Our biological rhythms can most clearly be seen in our monthly menstrual cycle. From our late teens to mid-thirties, there is a recurring ebb and flow of estrogen, progesterone, and testosterone that affects everything from our mood to our energy to our intuition.

Here is a week-by-week look:

- **Days 1-7:** With menstruation during the first few days and low levels of all sex hormones, we tend to feel tired and somewhat anti-social. As estrogen and testosterone begin to rise towards the end of this week, feel-good chemicals in the brain also increase and we start feeling energetic, confident, happy, and mentally alert.

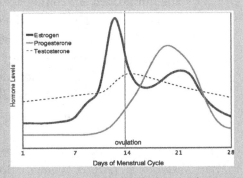

- **Days 8-14:** Estrogen and testosterone continue to rise along with feel-good brain chemicals, so we are at our peak for energy, mental alertness, happiness, motivation, athletic ability, and sex drive (just in time for ovulation). This week is the perfect time to start a new project or begin an exercise program.

- **Days 15-21:** Ovulation on day 14 triggers an increase in progesterone (the calming pregnancy hormone) to prepare for possible conception which has a dramatic dulling effect on our brain. Estrogen and testosterone levels drop and we tend to feel a bit sluggish and clumsy. We may feel emotionally vulnerable or a bit irritable and even notice a decline in our ability to communicate clearly. This week's effects of progesterone are similar to the "baby brain" phenomenon we experience during pregnancy.
- **Days 22-28:** During this premenstrual week, estrogen, progesterone, and testosterone take a plunge, and take our feel-good brain chemicals with them. We feel sapped of energy, irritable, and moody. Interestingly, our right brain becomes more active during this week, so we are more creative, intuitive, and inward-focused than at any other time in our cycle.

Sometime around our mid-thirties, our biological rhythms begin to change and lifestyle habits we got away with during our teens and twenties start to catch up with us.

- **Mid-Thirties-Late Forties:** The transition to menopause (*a.k.a.* **perimenopause**) begins during this time and our hormonal rhythms become somewhat erratic. Overall levels of the calming hormone progesterone begin to decrease and estrogen fluctuates up and down along with our feel-good brain chemicals. This can lead to a bumpy ride with issues such as mood swings, irritability, unprovoked anger and even rage, depression, anxiety, insomnia, weight gain, and foggy thinking. Overall testosterone levels are also decreasing which leads to feelings of fatigue, low sex drive, and diminished self-confidence. Combine all this with the day-to-day pressures and demands of motherhood and it's no wonder so many Moms are running on empty.
- **Fifties-Sixties:** During **menopause** the ebb and flow of sex hormones ceases as does our menstrual cycle. The energy and mood symptoms of perimenopause may persist as estrogen continues to fluctuate at low levels; however, once these fluctuations stop, we experience a renewed sense of creativity, intuition, and inner wisdom that we can use to serve our families and our communities.

Sources: Greene, R. (2005). Dr. Robert Greene's Perfect Balance. *New York: Three Rivers Press; Northrup, C. (2006).* Women's Bodies, Women's Wisdom. *New York: Bantam Dell.*

THE PATH TWO PHILOSOPHY

Before we jump into making lifestyle changes, it's important to remember that each of us is unique and there is no one-size-fits-all approach to our bodies, minds, and spirits, including our hormones. Every woman's hormonal balance, imbalances, and symptoms are different. You may experience depression, moodiness, and low energy when you're out of sync, while your best friend may feel revved up, anxious, and have trouble sleeping. You may have other friends still who experience minimal to no symptoms at all (try to love them anyway!). Each of us is different. This uniqueness also means that there is not a one-size-fits-all approach to restoring hormonal balance either. What works for your best friend or your sister may not work for you.

The Path Two philosophy for restoring your energy and mood is simple: Listen to your body. The hormone-related symptoms we experience are not just monthly or life stage-related annoyances, they are signals sent by our bodies to get our attention and let us know that we are out of balance. And according to women's hormone specialist, Dr. Robert Greene, the severity of our symptoms—the irritability, depression, fatigue, or anxiety—reflects the severity of the hormonal imbalance. Minor imbalances lead to subtle signs or "whispers" from your body, while more severe imbalances lead to louder signs or "hollers."

> **When you're suffering from burnout, *you* are the only person on earth who can help because you're the only one who can make the lifestyle changes that need to be made.**
>
> —Sarah Ban Breathnach

If you're dragging yourself through the day or on Mach 10 overdrive, losing it with your husband and children, and feeling like Jekyll and Hyde much of the time, know that your body is sending you a wake-up call—something in your life is out of sync and running on empty. Ignoring, denying, or wishing the signs away will not restore harmony to your hormones and your life. You are the only person who can do that for yourself. The following section will help you tune in to what your body is telling you so that you can address the imbalance and start feeling like the Mom and woman you want to be and are meant to be.

THE THREE F'S OF HORMONAL BALANCE

Based on my experience and research, I have found three keys to maintaining hormonal balance and our female fizziology. I call them the three F-words: Food, Fitness and Flow (by "flow" I mean the pace of our lives). I call these F-words because talk of "eating healthier," "exercising" or "slowing down" are most often taboo with running on empty Moms. They don't want to hear them!

However, I always find that once Moms understand these terms within the context of balancing our hormones and are able to experience their ability to restore our mood and energy, they very quickly change their minds.

And just to reassure you, we're not talking about a major lifestyle overhaul here. Making the adjustments needed to return to our natural hormonal rhythms can really be as simple as going back to the basics and asking ourselves: *What would a cavewoman do?*

Food: Replenishing our Bodies with Real Nutrients

Some time ago, I was grocery shopping with my children and we happened to check the ingredients on a product we needed to buy. Here's the list of ingredients: milk, bacterial culture, modified corn starch, propylene glycol mono fatty acid ester, color, cellulose gel and gum. Any idea what the product is? . . . It's sour cream. Baffling, isn't it? My kids thought these ingredients were a riot. For the duration of our shop, they would ask me to repeat the ingredients and then say: "Hey Mom! Do you want some propylene glycol mono fatty acid ester with that?!" I can pretty much guarantee that our cavewoman ancestors did not live on propylene glycol mono fatty acid ester and neither should we.

Now please understand that I am not suggesting we all start obsessing over reading food labels and what we eat. Living in fear and worry over food (or anything for that matter) is not a healthy choice. What I am suggesting is that we become more conscious about how we are nourishing ourselves, especially when it comes to our hormones, energy, and mood. I love the old adage: "If you've got garbage going in, you'll have garbage coming out." And if you're on empty feeling sluggish, grouchy, foggy, and frazzled, chances are you're not eating the most nutrient-rich foods for your body and hormones.

So, *what would a cavewoman do*?!

1. *Eat real food regularly.* Given that we still have the same metabolisms and physiologies as our hunter-gatherer ancestors, it's not surprising that we thrive on foods found in nature—fruits, vegetables, lean meats and fish, nuts, legumes, and whole grains. That triple shot latté may get you going first thing in the morning and that pre-packaged-microwave-on-high-for-15-minutes frozen dinner might get a meal on the table quickly at the end of the day, but it's these kinds of processed, nutrient-deficient foods that throw our hormonal mobiles off-kilter and eventually lead to running on empty.

Getting the nourishment our female bodies need for energy and mood involves eating a balance of protein, fat, and carbohydrates from natural sources, as you'll read in the following sections. It also involves eating these foods regularly throughout the day. All too often as Moms, we go to great lengths to feed our children healthy meals and snacks at regular intervals throughout the day, yet we do not take the time to do that for ourselves. And here's the problem when it comes to our hormones: skipping meals, eating on the go, or "grazing" on snacks throughout the day and evening causes roller coaster fluctuations in blood sugar and insulin levels that quickly lead to hormonal imbalance in the rest of our system. Eating balanced meals with the right carbohydrates, protein, and fat at regular intervals throughout the day is essential for stabilizing insulin and blood sugar levels.

Coffee is not a meal . . . even with milk.

—MIA LUNDIN

Reinvention Practice

ENERGY AND MOOD FROM A TO ZINC

In many cases, the running on empty and PMS symptoms we experience are related to deficiencies in certain vitamins and minerals that affect hormonal balance as well as energy and mood. Here are a few examples:

B-complex: B vitamins are depleted by the pill, stress, refined sugars, caffeine, alcohol, and hormonal transitions. Low levels of B vitamins lead to imbalances in estrogen and stress hormones as well as in certain brain chemicals that can lead to anxiety, nervous tension, and the whole gamut of PMS symptoms.

Iron: Low iron is common during the reproductive years if you menstruate heavily and/or are vegetarian. Iron deficiencies can result in fatigue, sluggishness, and mental fogginess.

Magnesium: Often referred to as the "anti-stress" mineral, magnesium has a calming, relaxing effect on the body. Low magnesium contributes to imbalances in estrogen and running on empty symptoms such as irritability, depression, anxiety, and insomnia. (Note: Craving chocolate can signal a lack of this important mineral.)

I have taken and recommended an age-appropriate women's multi-vitamin for many years and know first-hand the benefits of increased energy and fewer PMS and other symptoms related to hormonal imbalance. Worth a try, don't you think?!

Sources: Northrup, C. (2006). Women's Bodies, Women's Wisdom. *New York: Bantam Dell. Lundin, M. (2009).* Female Brain Gone Insane. *Deerfield Beach: Health Communications, Inc.*

---

2. *Avoid hormone chaos carbs.* According to medical and health experts, one of the biggest hormone epidemics in North America today is too much insulin from too many hormone chaos carbs. Chaos carbs are the refined sugars and processed ingredients found in white bread and pasta, instant rice, cereals, cookies, cakes and other baked goods made with white flour, sodas, and juice drinks. These refined foods cause drastic surges and drops in blood sugar that throw off the entire hormonal system leaving us fatigued, moody, and constantly hungry, specifically for more chaos carbs.

Healthy or unrefined carbohydrates, on the other hand, come from natural whole foods such as vegetables, fruits, and grains. The fiber in these carbs helps prevent the roller coaster fluctuations in insulin and blood sugar levels and actually contributes to hormonal balance in our bodies. These foods provide quality fuel, helping to boost energy levels, maintain mental clarity, and curb hunger and cravings throughout the day.

In the spirit of our cavewoman ancestors, I'd like to add one final word on chaos carbs and sugar. Recent research has shown that our hunter-gatherer ancestors ate the equivalent of only twenty teaspoons of sugar *a year*. Other than the occasional honey, sugar was simply not available. Today, we eat more than twenty teaspoons of sugar *a day*. A day! Added sugar is everywhere from yogurt, juice, bread, and cereal to seemingly harmless condiments such as ketchup and mayonnaise. And of course it's at the checkout counter, within arms reach, at every supermarket and convenience store we shop at. It's no wonder obesity, diabetes, and brain disorders, not to mention hormonal imbalances, have become such an epidemic in our culture. Our bodies have not evolved the way the food industry has.

If you want to be depressed, tired, anxious, hyperactive but unfocused, and lose your memory . . . then keep eating sugar.
—Dr. Mark Hyman

As Moms and women who do the majority of the meal planning and food shopping in our households, we are in a powerful position to impact the health and understanding our children and families have when it comes to the foods we eat. Don't underestimate the sugar content of the foods you buy or the effects of sugar on our health and well-being. And let's ensure our children are just as informed.

3. *Get enough protein.* Most women do not get enough protein to properly fuel their bodies and brains. Grabbing quick meals and eating on-the-go means that we tend to eat a lot of low fat, high carb foods (as do our children), most of which are not always the healthiest carbohydrates—cereal, breakfast bars, bagels, muffins, pasta made with white flour, etc. Proteins are the building blocks of our bodies and are essential for producing hormones, energy, and stamina. Without enough protein from the foods we eat, our bodies and brains quickly become sluggish.

   In her book, *A Smart Woman's Guide to Hormones*, leading women's health expert, Lorna Vanderhaeghe, emphasizes the importance of eating protein at every meal. "Your plate should have forty percent protein, with the balance of the plate filled with lots of colorful vegetables and good fats," says Vanderhaeghe. Rich sources of protein come from both animals and plants including lean meats such as poultry, fresh fish, eggs, soy, legumes, seeds, nuts, and dairy.

   While I certainly appreciate and respect animal rights and environmental concerns regarding the eating of animal foods, I believe this decision is an individual choice. Some women do well on vegetarian and vegan diets, while others do not. I am a big advocate of trying out different approaches to healthy eating and determining which one(s) work best for you. How do certain foods feel in your body after you've eaten them? Which foods help you feel energized and mentally sharp and which ones make you feel sluggish and foggy? Whether you choose a vegan, vegetarian, or flexitarian approach when it comes to protein, and all foods for that matter, the most important thing you can do is find an approach that makes you feel happy, vital, and healthy and go with it.

4. *Eat healthy fats.* Yes, fats are our friends. The right kind of fats, that is. We have a whole slew of bad fats to contend with due to the refining and processing of foods today. It's no secret that saturated, hydrogenated, and trans fats are the culprits when it comes to heart disease and other health problems. They also contribute to hormonal imbalance. What you may not know is that polyunsaturated fats, particularly omega-3, are essential to the health and well-being of our female bodies.

   Omega-3 fats (found in fish, dark green leafy vegetables, flaxseed, and walnuts) are essential to the optimal functioning of every cell membrane in the body. Getting sufficient amounts of this nutrient helps prevent fatigue, depression, PMS, hormonal imbalances, menstrual cramps, breast tenderness, achy joints and arthritis, not to mention the tremendous benefits it has for cardiovascular health.

5. *Limit caffeine and alcohol.* I know, I know. Whenever I mention this one, I hear the gasps and groans from Moms! Coffee and wine are staples for many a Mom's long, busy days. Unfortunately, excessive caffeine and alcohol consumption are at the top of running on empty Moms' lists for habits that are counterproductive to hormonal balance.

While there is some evidence showing that coffee and wine may be beneficial in moderation, you'll need to tune in to your own body's wisdom to determine what "moderation" is for you. I personally love coffee, but I have become increasingly sensitive to the effects of caffeine as I've entered the perimenopausal stage of life. Specifically, I noticed a lot of irritability and anger premenstrually as well as a grogginess upon waking when I was drinking caffeine throughout the day. I now try to limit myself to one cup of coffee or green tea in the morning and then drink herbal tea or lemon water throughout the rest of the day. Since making this change, my hormonal symptoms have decreased dramatically. Interestingly, I've also noticed that my dreams are much more vivid and memorable.

Alcohol has similar effects on disrupting mood and sleep as well as worsening PMS symptoms. It acts as a depressant, temporarily sedating the brain, which is why most women enjoy a glass of wine or two at the end of the day—it calms them down and helps them unwind. However, its high sugar content and effects on the liver also affect insulin and estrogen which contributes to hormonal imbalance. If you feel the need to have a few drinks in the evening (or an entire bottle of wine as one Mom shared with me) in order to relax and unwind, I would suggest examining your lifestyle and relationship to alcohol. There are far better ways to unwind at the end of the day, even with children at home: relaxing music, a cup of tea, or a hot shower to name a few.

> **I'm on a gin and tonic diet. So far I've lost two days.**
> —ANONYMOUS

Many women don't begin experiencing hormonal sensitivities to food, caffeine, and alcohol until into their thirties when our eating habits from our teens and twenties start to catch up with us. And by the time we reach the hormonal transitions of perimenopause in our later thirties and forties, the vast majority of us will feel the effects of our daily food choices on our mood and energy. This certainly doesn't mean that we can't ever have coffee or wine or indulge in our guilty pleasures. I have found (and many health experts recommend) that if you stick with a healthy balance of carbs, protein, and fats from natural food sources eighty percent of the time, you'll still have room to indulge.

Again, take some time to experiment with the foods you eat and see how they affect your running on empty and hormonal symptoms. Eliminate or cut back on one food at a time such as caffeine, alcohol, sugar, meat, white breads and pasta. Stick with the change for a month or two to see how your body, energy, and mood respond. You might be surprised at what you discover.

Fitness: Moving Our Bodies to Restore Energy and Mood

Let me preface this section by saying that by "fitness" I don't mean specialized cardio training or passing standards of strength and endurance. For our purposes, fitness simply means "moving your body," so please don't let the term scare you off. I chose "fitness" merely because I needed an F-word!

Hands down, fitness is right at the top of the list with food when it comes to hormone balance. If you think about what our cavewoman ancestors would have done, they would have spent their days being physically active—gathering food, carrying water, and walking wherever they and their families needed to go. Back then, they called this activity survival. Today we call it "working out." Our bodies are meant to move, plain and simple. And all the systems in our body, including our hormones and brain, function best when we're active.

I know that moving your body is the last thing you want to hear when you're running on empty. Most Moms would rather put on a pair of pajamas then a pair of running shoes. I hope that understanding fitness within the context of balancing your hormones and restoring your energy and mood will help you reconsider your relationship to your running shoes.

Fitness, Hormones, and Fizziology

I don't have to tell you about all the wonderful benefits of exercise. We are smart, educated women. We know the benefits and have even experienced most of them for ourselves. But if you're like the majority of Moms who know these benefits and still aren't physically active, then you may not understand the relationship between fitness and hormones. Understanding how physical activity affected my own hormonal balance, including my mood, energy, and sanity, is the key factor that got me and keeps me active. Let's take a look at the hormonal benefits of fitness when it comes to our female fizziology:

- *Fitness lowers stress hormones and releases "feel good" brain chemicals.* When we're running around in a constant state of doing, our bodies become chronically stressed. The stress hormones cortisol and adrenaline are pumped through our bodies to keep us ready for action, increasing our heart rate and blood sugar, diverting blood flow away from our brain and into our muscles, and disconnecting us from how we feel. This is what keeps us running on auto-pilot and adrenaline. Over time, these chronically elevated levels of stress hormones throw off the rest of our hormonal mobile and cause us to feel fatigued, listless, and mentally foggy. Getting your body moving counteracts this state of stress by initiating the *relaxation response.* This response stabilizes stress hormones and releases feel good brain chemicals (called serotonin and endorphins) that boost our energy and our sense of well-being and pleasure. The relaxation response also helps us sleep better—we sleep more soundly and for less periods of time.

- *Fitness benefits sex hormones.* As we saw in the "Our Life in Hormones" section earlier, our bodies begin to produce less testosterone and estrogen as we age. The good news is that regular fitness can help slow this age-related process. According to Dr. Greene, exercise boosts our testosterone levels by as much as fifteen percent which improves energy and mood, not to mention confidence, sex drive, and weight loss. Staying active also normalizes estrogen levels in our bodies which aids in our overall hormonal balance and in alleviating PMS and running on empty symptoms.
- *Fitness improves brain functioning.* Because of all the rich connections and constant activity in our female brain, we require significantly more blood flow to the brain than our male counterparts. Moving our bodies increases this blood flow and allows us to think much more clearly and efficiently than when we're running on empty. It also allows us greater access to our intuition.

The bottom line is clear: Being physically active is essential to offsetting the sluggishness, moodiness, and fogginess of running on empty. There are no ifs, ands, or buts about it. And trust me, I know all the ifs, ands, or buts there are when it comes to fitness. I've heard them all and have used many of them myself: "I don't have time," "I hate exercise," and "Ugghh, I don't have the energy." These excuses come from the running on empty voice speaking on our behalf and the only thing we can do is rise above it and get moving anyway.

> **Align with the feeling that tells you: "This is the right thing to do."**
> —Dr. Wayne W. Dyer

I have come to think about fitness much like I do brushing my teeth or taking a shower: It's not terribly exciting, but if you don't do it, life becomes out of sorts and intolerable. And not just for you, but for everyone around you as well. When you start thinking about fitness as a kind of "hormonal hygiene," you stop making excuses and just take the time to do it.

Your fitness routine doesn't have to be anything fancy or complex. Tune in to your body's wisdom and choose activities that make you feel good. Some women find walking or yoga great forms of fitness. For them, these activities several times a week keep them feeling great. Others need to exert more energy and find competitive sports or other forms of cardio such as running, swimming, or biking are necessary to give them the boost they need. Finding something that works for you and feels right for your body is the way to go when it comes to staying physically active.

Many women (myself included) find it difficult to stick with their fitness routine—they either get bored or fall back into running on empty excuses. In this case, consider pairing up with a friend or joining a group. I see pairs of Moms jogging, groups of Moms doing stroller fitness, and even some learning pole dancing together (or so I hear!) all the time. And if you think about it, cavewomen would have done the same thing (not the pole dancing, but the activity in groups). Our ancestors moved together for the greater purpose of ensuring survival through hunting, gathering, and resettling, as well as for togetherness through sport and dance. In this spirit, many women find it helpful to have a greater purpose they are active for—running for a cause, biking for charity, or walking for awareness of an important issue. Moving our bodies for a greater purpose can often provide the extra boost we need to stay committed to a physically active lifestyle.

And if you can get your children involved in your fitness activity in some way, that's even better. We have an increasing crisis in our culture of overweight, under-active children, so modeling a positive, healthy approach to looking after our bodies and minds will make a big difference for our selves as well as for generations to come.

The Mommy Diaries

WHAT I KNOW FOR SURE

A few years ago, I started feeling unusually sluggish and tired. All the time. Even with two young girls and a full-time job, I knew there was something more to my lack of energy than just being a busy mom and career woman. I realized I had to make some changes the day my oldest daughter said, "Mommy, why are you so tired all the time?" That was a big wake-up call for me. Not only was my lack of energy affecting my ability to get through each day, it was also affecting my girls' perception of their mom.

I made the conscious decision to start taking the time to recharge and re-energize, not by heading to the nearest spa (which was my first thought!) but by getting my body moving. I decided to start running—an inexpensive, convenient form of working out. Taking this time allows me to clear my head and gives me the energy I need to do all that I do each day. I also feel like I'm being a more positive role model for my girls. I want my daughters to grow up appreciating the energy they get from exercising and loving and respecting their bodies. Without the well-being and energy you get from recharging your body, I know for sure, you simply can't be the mom you want to be.

Eryn, Mom of two and executive assistant

Flow: Slowing Down to the Speed of Life

Most of the Moms I work with are either so busy that they rarely have time to just sit and relax or so exhausted from all their doing that they can't fathom doing one more thing. In addition to poor food and fitness habits, these tendencies stem from an inability to listen to our bodies and replenish ourselves with appropriate downtime—an inability that eventually catches up with us in the form of burnout or illness.

While it's easy to get caught up in all the doing and push ourselves to do more as Moms and women, this approach to living keeps us in a state of stress where our bodies are constantly flooded with stress hormones. And as we've already learned, these elevated stress levels eventually lead to hormonal imbalance in the rest of our body and to running on empty. Tuning in to our body's wisdom and respecting its natural rhythms can help us slow down, reduce our stress hormones, and restore our bodies to a state of well-being.

The Wisdom of Our Bodies

Currently there is an advertisement for a feminine hygiene product that uses the slogan: "Kick mother nature to the curb." Mother Nature seems to get a lot of that these days. With all the advances in science and medicine over the last one hundred years, our culture has strived to control many of the natural bodily processes we find inconvenient rather than tune in to the messages and wisdom our bodies offer us. A good example of this is the recent advances in birth control pills that allow for only a few "scheduled" periods a year or that even eliminate periods altogether. We want to control the things that we see as annoyances and prevent us from all of our doing. But the truth is that respecting and restoring our body's natural rhythms rather than kicking them to the curb, will go a heck of a lot further in allowing us to do all of our doing with more energy and wisdom. It will even enable us to do some being, too.

> **The ebb and flow of hormones . . . offers us a profound opportunity to deepen our connection with our inner knowing.**
>
> —CHRISTIANE NORTHRUP, M.D.

Remember the graph in the "Our Life in Hormones" section earlier in this chapter that showed the ebb and flow of our hormones on a monthly basis? You may recall that this monthly rhythm reflects not only the ups and downs of our sex hormones, but also the ups and downs of our energy and mood. These natural ebbs and flows provide us with deep wisdom about when to focus our energy externally to get things done and when to shift our focus internally and slow things down. In her book, *Women's Bodies, Women's Wisdom*, Dr. Christiane Northrup beautifully describes the anatomy of this monthly wisdom . . .

Many women find that they are at their peak of expression in the outer world from the onset of their menstrual cycle until ovulation. Their energy is outgoing and upbeat. They are filled with enthusiasm and new ideas as well as being quite willing to fold the towels and fulfill their perceived role of helping others. . . .

If we do not become biologically pregnant at ovulation, we move into the second half of the cycle . . . ovulation through the onset of menstruation. During this phase we quite naturally retreat from outward activity to a more reflective mode. . . . We turn more inward, preparing *to develop or give birth to something that comes from deep within ourselves.* . . .

[This second phase], from ovulation until the onset of menstruation, is when women *are most in tune with their inner knowing and with what isn't working in their lives.*

We need not be afraid or think we are sick if our energies and moods naturally ebb for a few days each month. . . . I have come to see that all kinds of stress-related disease, ranging from PMS to osteoporosis, could be lessened a great deal if we simply followed our body's wisdom once per month. (excerpts from 105-107)

These premenstrual energies, emotions, and inward moods are very difficult for us to accept. We see them as nuisances and unproductive. The very idea of slowing down and resting is a foreign concept to most of us. We feel like we *need to* and *should* be doing something. We feel guilty about taking downtime for ourselves when there's laundry to do, groceries to buy, and errands to be done. But we need to believe in the importance of the messages our bodies send us. If we ignore our biology and fight our own nature, our bodies have little choice but to speak louder to us in the form of running on empty and PMS symptoms. When we respect and honor this wisdom, we stay within the flow and natural rhythms that lead to internal balance and well-being.

Of course, in addition to this monthly wisdom, there is much daily wisdom to be gleaned as well: taking a much needed break, getting sufficient amounts of sleep, and taking downtime at the end of the day and week. I know all too well that downtime and sleep are difficult when you have little ones at home with you. Heck, some days it's a challenge to even go to the bathroom! While these challenges certainly lessen as your children get older, it's still essential to develop the habit of taking time to let everything go and just relax. Downtime can be anything from a walk or a hot bath to a few extra moments to enjoy a cup of tea or sleep in. Remember that these are some of the same practices we discussed in Path One for stepping to the right and quieting the mind. By slowing down, we not only tune in to our feminine wisdom, but also replenish our bodies by lowering stress hormones and restoring our fizziology.

Sometimes the most important thing in a whole day is the rest we take between two breaths.

—François de la Rochefoucauld

And when it comes to sleep, it helps to think like our ancestors who would have slept eight to ten hours a night as they went to bed and woke with the sun. They would have gone to bed without the effects of caffeine or the glowing screens of computers or TV which interfere with the hormone melatonin—a regulatory hormone that is critical to the normal sleep-wake cycle. And they would have slept in a calm, peaceful environment surrounded by the sounds of nature. Optimizing our sleep in these ways restores our energy and improves our mood and mental clarity.

Reinvention Practice

WAITING TO INHALE

In her book, *Consciously Female*, Tracey Gaudet, M.D., points out that when we're constantly doing and focusing outside of ourselves, it's a lot like exhaling all of the time—doing our jobs, managing our homes, nurturing relationships, helping with homework, getting to soccer. Breathing out, out, out, virtually 24/7. If you actually try breathing that way for a moment, you'll find very quickly that you run out of steam. You're on empty.

We are all waiting to inhale. We're in desperate need of getting oxygen and learning how to slow down so we can breathe in *and* breathe out. While the suggestion of breathing may sound trite, it actually has many benefits for our physical and emotional well-being. Taking several slow, deep breaths triggers the relaxation response in our bodies which lowers our stress hormones, heart rate, and blood pressure and induces a feeling of calmness. By restoring our inner physiology in this way, we also transform the energy we have to send out into the world—to our children, our partner, our home, our work, and our community.

Take time during the day to focus on breathing in *and* breathing out. When you're frazzled and overwhelmed, stop and take a moment to breathe in and out. When you find yourself on the verge of a meltdown, inhale and exhale deeply. It won't solve everything, but it is a solid step towards replenishing and reconnecting.

As you begin to incorporate food, fitness, and flow—the three F's—into your reinvention journey, you will discover more vitality, improved moods, and a better ability to "go with the flow." You will even find that your patience and tolerance for frustration increases dramatically. And we all know how critical our patience levels are when you have children! Often times when Moms restore their energy and mood, they forget or don't realize how far they've come. I suggest writing down your running on empty feelings and symptoms in your journal before you get started and keep track of your progress every couple of weeks or so. You'll be amazed at how much better you feel and you'll have a good reminder about life on empty if you start to fall off "the reinvention wagon!"

While it's easy to see the impact that food, fitness, and flow have on our female fizziologies, it's also important to maintain perspective and not get caught up in obsessing over your health. Sometimes when we get too eager about taking care of our body, we begin to treat it as a machine or functional "thing" that requires twenty minutes of this three times a week and fifty milligrams of that each day. The human body is one of nature's greatest masterpieces and finding ways to take pleasure in and be grateful for it—exactly as it was designed for you—is just as essential to our health and well-being. Our thoughts about loving and accepting our bodies versus disliking and ignoring them will affect us in very different ways, right down to the cellular level of our being. If you can begin Path Two with appreciation and love for your body, you'll have a wonderful head start.

> **Loving ourselves is the miracle cure we are all looking for.**
> —Louise Hay

*   *   *   *   *

One of my favourite authors and speakers, Dr. Wayne Dyer, wisely reminds us of the following: *"You've been provided with a perfect body to house your soul for a few brief moments in eternity. So regardless of its size, shape, color, or any imagined infirmities, you can honor the temple that houses you by eating healthfully, exercising, listening to your body's needs, and treating it with dignity and love."* Couldn't have said it better myself. Let the F-words begin!

REFLECTION AND ACTION FOR PATH TWO

- ✄ Give yourself some time to tune in to and discover your natural hormonal rhythms. What do you notice? If you have a daughter, how can you help her discover and honor her hormonal rhythms?

- ✄ Consider your current thoughts, beliefs, and habits around food, fitness, and flow. Are you addicted to sugary foods, refined carbohydrates, caffeine, and/or alcohol? Do you include protein with every meal? Do you have ready-made excuses about why you can't be physically active? Does the thought of slowing down and resting make you feel uncomfortable or guilty? Examining your relationship to each of the three F's will help you determine where to focus your attention on this pathway.

Kelly Pryde, Ph.D.

✂ What messages—either conscious or unconscious—do you send your body? Do you love and nurture it or do you focus on the things you don't like and neglect it with poor lifestyle choices? You might try looking in the mirror and smiling at yourself as you remember these words from poet Carolyn Rogers: *"And one day I took a good long look at myself in a full-length mirror . . . and I knew that many things were over and some me of beauty was about to begin."*

FURTHER READING FOR PATH TWO

Women's Bodies, Women's Wisdom by Christiane Northrup, M.D. (New York: Bantam Dell, 2006)

A staple for every woman's bookshelf, this visionary book draws together conventional medicine and natural remedies to offer women mind-body-spirit wellness for every aspect of their bodies and lives.

Dr. Robert Greene's Perfect Balance by Robert A. Greene, M.D. and Leah Feldon. (New York: Three Rivers Press, 2005)

One of North America's leading hormone specialists explains how hormonal balance can significantly improve women's health and quality of life.

Consciously Female: How to Listen to Your Body and Soul for a Lifetime of Healthier Living by Tracey W. Gaudet, M.D. (New York: Bantam Dell, 2004)

Draws on conventional and alternative medicine to explain how women can reconnect their bodies and souls by better understanding the inner workings of their bodies and their feminine wisdom.

Mom Energy: A Simple Plan to Live Fully Charged by Ashley Koff, R.D. and Kathy Kaehler (Carlsbad, CA: Hay House, 2011)

A dietician and fitness trainer duo offer a practical and flexible program to help Moms increase their energy levels through a simple three-step process: reorganize, rehabilitate, and recharge.

PATH 3

EMOTIONAL FENG SHUI

Rearranging Your Emotional House

Years ago when my daughter was in Junior Kindergarten, she had come home from school and was sitting in the kitchen telling me about her day. As I talked with her and unpacked her lunch bag, I noticed that she hadn't eaten the sandwich I made for her. "Honey, you didn't eat your sandwich today?" I asked curiously. With a look of disgust, she said, "No, Mom. Look at it." I opened the sandwich container and was horrified to find a big green patch of mold on the corner of the bread. Uggghhh. Immediately, the wheels started spinning in my mind as I wondered, no, panicked, about who had seen this atrocity of a sandwich. "Honey, I am so sorry. Did someone tell you not to eat it or did you just know not to?" I asked rather craftily. "Oh, I just knew not to eat it," she said. Phew! I felt a huge wave of relief wash over me.

As I proceeded to throw the sandwich away, I once again apologized to this poor little 4-year-old for my incompetent sandwich making. "Honey, I really am sorry I did that and ruined your lunch. That green stuff is called mold." She nodded matter-of-factly and shrugged, "Yeah, that's what Mrs. Cona said."

Whenever I share that story with fellow Moms, their immediate reaction is laughter followed by empathy: "Aw. That could've happened to anyone" and "What an unfortunate mistake." But inevitably after a few moments, most Moms will admit that while they are able to empathize with my story, they know that they would have been berating themselves, feeling guilty, and worrying about what others were thinking about them for days had they done that themselves. Sound familiar?!

As Moms and women, we are notorious for hanging on to "emotional clutter." Feelings such as guilt, worry, fear, resentment, and depression are commonplace in our emotional repertoires. We feel guilty about losing it on our kids, wanting time alone, and not always being

> **Our fatigue is often caused not by work, but by worry, frustration, and resentment.**
>
> —DALE CARNEGIE

the Moms we want to be. We worry about doing all the right things and giving our children the best advantages in life and we feel guilty when we think we haven't done that for them. We resent looking after everyone else's needs while no one takes care of ours. We feel depressed and hopeless that the constant to-do's and running around is all there is and we feel guilty for wanting more. Yes, there is a lot of emotional clutter in the mommy mind.

While being emotional is part of our feminine nature, as we learned in the first pathway, most of us have never learned how to process all of these feelings in healthy ways—we either rationalize or stuff them away and put on a happy face so we can keep going or we allow them to hang around while we ruminate and obsess over the thoughts that play over and over again in our minds. Either way, all of these unprocessed emotions begin to accumulate and form what I call "emotional clutter zones." Over time, all this clutter wears us down and starts to fester in our minds and bodies.

In feng shui terms (pronounced "fung shway" in case you were wondering), emotional clutter is low, stagnant energy that will not only drain us of our energy and pull us into a running on empty state, but also set us up for risk of physical disease if we don't process it and clear it out (see "The Anatomy of Emotional Dis-Ease" section below). The effects of emotional clutter are much like walking into a room or closet that is overflowing with boxes and piles of unwanted, unmanaged items—it feels overwhelming and chaotic and "heavy." It becomes exhausting having all this stuff weigh down on us. But as we all know when we finally decide to de-clutter our spaces, we don't just start grabbing everything and tossing it to the curb. We sort through things. We examine them. We think about each item and make the determination: Is there some value in this? In this way, some items will go promptly into the junk pile, while others can be quite valuable if we look at them in a new way. This is the same approach to take in processing our thoughts and feelings as well.

Contrary to what we have learned over the last two decades with the emphasis on positive psychology and optimism, there really are no negative emotions. The emotions we call "negative"—guilt, worry, fear, frustration, anger, depression—are energies that are trying to get our attention to give us information and impel us to action. The only thing negative is how we think about and respond to the emotions and experiences we don't like. We think, "I'm a terrible mother," "I should be doing more," "I don't have time for this," "I do everything around here. It's so unfair," "I can't take this

> **There are no negative emotions; there are only negative attitudes toward emotions we don't like and can't tolerate, and the negative consequences of denying them.**
>
> —Miriam Greenspan

anymore." These are the kinds of thoughts and beliefs that contribute to most of our emotional clutter. Our negative attitudes and reactions are what drain us of our emotional energy and keep us stuck in a running on empty way of living.

The Anatomy of Emotional Dis-Ease

THE EFFECTS OF EMOTIONAL CLUTTER IN THE BODY

For hundreds of years, medical practitioners have observed that certain emotions appear to be related to certain illnesses and parts of the body. Understanding this connection can help us identify emotional issues we might need to resolve. Here are a few examples:

Emotional Dis-ease	Physical Symptoms
• fear, stress, anxiety, control issues (e.g., perfectionism, over-achievement) related to self-esteem and feelings of inadequacy, substance abuse	intestinal problems, adrenal dysfunction, ulcers, weight issues, indigestion, heartburn, irritable bowel syndrome
• not speaking up for oneself; repressed or "swallowed" anger; imbalance between determination & patience	thyroid issues, chronic sore throats, chronic neck pain
• "stuffed emotions;" unresolved anger & grief; bitterness & resentment; lack of joy	heart disease, high cholesterol, hypertension, chest pain
• lack of nurturance from self & others; self-sacrificing; imbalance between giving & receiving; guilt	breast issues (e.g., cysts, tumors), lung problems (e.g., asthma), pneumonia

Sources: Schulz, M.L. (2010), The Intuitive Advisor. *Carlsbad, CA: Hay House; Myss, C. (1996),* Anatomy of the Spirit. *New York: Three Rivers Press; Colbert, D. (2006),* Deadly Emotions. *Nashville: Thomas Nelson.*

Consider my moldy sandwich story, for example. Did I feel guilty when I found out that I had sent my child to school with a moldy sandwich? You bet I did. I felt terrible. Did I marinate in the guilt for hours, feeling like a terrible mother and worrying about what the lunchtime supervisor was thinking and telling the other teachers? While there certainly was a time when I would have reacted that way, I didn't. What good would that have done? How would that have helped my daughter in that moment or in the future? That's not what the guilty

> **There's no word in Tibetan for 'guilty.' The closest thing is 'intelligent regret that decides to do things differently.'**
>
> —GESHE MICHAEL ROACH

feelings were there to tell me. The guilt was simply alerting me to the fact that I had done something wrong, that an apology was in order, and that it would be a good idea to be more careful with my sandwich-making practices in the future. End of story. Unfortunately, we have learned to attach so many negative thoughts and beliefs around things that go wrong and that we don't like that we create a lot of emotional chaos and clutter for ourselves as a result.

Until today.

On this pathway, we'll explore how the emotional issues and experiences that clutter our minds and deplete us are actually our biggest windows into restoring our emotional energy and reconnecting to our inner guidance. Once we realize that all of our emotions are purposeful and useful, we can begin to listen to them and act on them in ways that are healthy, loving, and wise. We don't need to "conquer" any feelings or eliminate them. We simply need to identify and re-arrange the way we think about and respond to our emotional experiences. All it takes is a little understanding and a little feng shui in our emotional house.

Reinvention Practice

LETTING GO OF GUILT

Guilt is one of the most prevalent emotional issues with Moms. Unfortunately, it's also one of the greatest wastes of time and emotional energy. Here's how to turn that wasted energy into something much more productive for both you and your family . . .

Consider Guilt: Guilt is an inner signal telling us we've done something wrong—something that either goes against our values or against our idea of how things "should" be. It offers us an opportunity for change by telling us to "pay attention to what's happened here and learn from it." Then we can let go and move on. But most of us rarely resolve guilt in this "learn and let go" way. Instead, we ruminate over how horrible we feel and we use up all of our present moments blaming and judging ourselves for something that is over and done with—something we can never change. This is guilt gone awry.

Learn and Let Go: When guilty feelings come up, simply ask yourself: "Did I make a mistake I can learn from here or am I being too hard on myself?" Then, either change your future behavior or change how you're thinking about the situation. Feeling guilty about missing your child's school play is a valid cue to change your time management practices in the future. Pay attention, Mom! Feeling guilty about not ironing the bed sheets is a sure sign to change your thinking. Lighten up, Mom!

Making mistakes is part and parcel of being a parent and we will continue to make them—some big and some insignificant. Letting go of guilt along with self blame, judgment, and criticism is key to learning and growing and, more importantly, to becoming a more loving person.

DE-CLUTTERING THE MOMMY MIND

Over the years, my own personal experience and my experience working with fellow Moms has led me to identify several common areas where we have misdirected thoughts and stagnant emotional energy. I call these emotional clutter zones. These clutter zones have built up over the years from painful emotions we have stuffed away from our past, from misguided thoughts about ourselves, and from erroneous beliefs about how things "should" be. Here are the five most common emotional clutter zones for Moms:

- **Tyrannical Self-Talk**: speaking to ourselves in ways that are critical and toxic to our emotional and psychological well-being.
- **Perfectionism**: having a strong need to maintain ideal (sometimes impossible) standards as a parent and in other areas of life.
- **Übermom Syndrome**: living and parenting by the "I can do it all" maxim.
- **Stuck in Pissosity**: having a strong tendency to blame, judge, criticize, and complain about things that don't go the way we think they should.
- **Something More:** experiencing a nagging doubt or sadness that something is missing in our lives.

Once we recognize these clutter zones in our emotional house, we can choose to listen to the wisdom our feelings offer us and clear out any unhelpful or toxic thoughts and beliefs with the help of some simple practices. Let's take a closer look at each of the five emotional clutter zones and explore some ways to feng shui the mind.

1. Tyrannical Self-Talk

By far, Moms are their own worst enemies when it comes to their self-talk. The words and tone of voice we use to speak to ourselves are often riddled with judgment and criticism which, not surprisingly, leads to a lot of emotional stress and turmoil.

This kind of negative self-talk stems from our inner critic (that left-brain chatterbox we discussed in the first pathway) and is so well-developed and automatic that most Moms rarely notice it's there. But if you pay attention to how you speak to yourself, you'll notice the harshness of this tyrannical ruler. It uses words like *should, have to* and *need to*. It sets up a lot of "musts" in our minds. When we take this approach, we tell ourselves things like: "I should be spending more time with my kids," "I shouldn't be eating this," "I have to do the laundry," "I need to be more organized." I should, I have to, I need to. I must.

While the goal of our tyrannical self-talk is often well-intended—we really just want to be good Moms and people—the way in which we go about it creates a lot of emotional clutter. Firstly, telling ourselves that we "have to" or "must" do something eliminates our right to choose. We actually render ourselves powerless against our own self. And because we believe that our musts are so important and highly valued, we put a lot of pressure on ourselves to get all these things done. When and if they don't get done, we feel guilty and beat ourselves up for not following through on these ever-so-important to-dos. Talk about emotionally draining.

> **The shoulds always produce a feeling of strain, which is all the greater the more a person tries to actualize [her] shoulds in [her] behavior.**
> —Dr. Karen Horney

Secondly, when we "should" ourselves, we are unconsciously telling our selves that what we are currently doing is not good enough—a message that only serves to diminish our sense of self and our emotional well-being. Who needs that?! Being a recovering self-should-er myself I know first-hand how draining and disheartening it is to constantly should all over yourself. And while I'm very careful not to should myself anymore, I occasionally catch myself shoulding my children. Unfortunately, this is where I learned a very powerful lesson on the impact of this one little word.

My daughter, who was ten at the time, has extremely curly hair. It's the kind of hair that must be "picked" instead of combed or brushed and requires a really good conditioner in order to get a comb through it following a shower. Ever since she's had hair, I've helped her manage and groom these remarkable curls. As she got older, however, I wanted her to start learning how to properly care for her own hair. Unfortunately, my desire for this came out one evening after a long, trying day when my tolerance for frustration was particularly low.

As I was struggling to comb through her hair after her shower that night, I was complaining that she hadn't properly conditioned it, pointing out all the tangles and knots that were impossible to comb. Upon realizing that *I* would need to re-condition her hair for the *third* time that week in order to properly comb it, I lost my cool and blurted out, "You're ten years old! You need to be more responsible for looking after your own hair. I shouldn't have to condition your hair again for you so that it can be combed. You should be doing it properly in the shower." As soon as the words left my mouth, my daughter's head and shoulders just slumped. It was as if someone—me in this case—had let the air out of her upper body. My barrage of "need tos" and "shoulds" had completely deflated her.

> Handle them carefully, for words have more power than atom bombs.
>
> —Pearl Strachan Hurd

This incident was the biggest eye-opener for me on the powerful impact of these tyrannical words—they hurt, they disempower, and they belittle. We don't need this kind of energy in our emotional house. We deserve so much more than that, as do our children. With that in mind, here are some ways to feng shui this tyrannical self-talk . . .

FENG SHUI SOLUTIONS FOR TYRANNICAL SELF-TALK

- **Pay attention to your self-talk.** Most Moms don't realize how often they use "shoulds," "have tos," and "need tos" when speaking to themselves and others. We always get a good laugh during my seminars when we discuss this topic because inevitably Moms will offer ideas and ask questions using the word "should." Chances are you use these tyrannical terms a lot more than you think you do, too. Once you've identified this emotional clutter, you can begin to clear it out.

- **Toss "shoulds," "musts," "need tos," and "have tos" to the curb.** It's pretty clear that these words can go straight to the junk pile. No matter which way you look at them, there is little value in keeping these terms in our vocabularies. Instead, try replacing these tyrannical terms with emotionally fueling phrases such as "I would like to" and "I am going to." For example, instead of saying: "I should exercise more often" and "I need to do the laundry," which inevitably leads to feelings of guilt and defeat, try saying: "I'd like to exercise more often" and "I'm going to do the laundry." These latter versions are a much kinder, gentler way of speaking to ourselves and lead to a much more constructive frame of mind. Try saying these different phrases to yourself—the tyrannical ones and the feng shui'd ones—and see if you can feel the difference in your energy.

- **Remember this mantra:** *"Don't should on yourself. Don't should on other people. And don't let other people should on you."* Wise words to live by! Almost everyone has a should-er in her life. Aside from yourself, it could be a spouse, ex, parent, mother-in-law, or friend. Until today they probably have been driving you crazy and draining a lot of your emotional energy. Now that you understand that these "shoulds" are simply a result of their own emotional clutter, you'll be far less likely to be bothered by them. When someone shoulds on you, you can chuckle to yourself and simply respond with "Thanks, I'll consider that" or "That's an interesting idea." End of tyranny.

The Mommy Diaries

SHOULDING ALL OVER MYSELF

I have a lot of trouble with the word "should." I can really send myself into a frenzy over all the stuff I think I "should" be doing. Sometimes I tell myself I "should" get up earlier so I have more time to get things done. I also think I "should" do a better job staying on top of my family's laundry. We rummage through laundry baskets more often than dresser drawers!

But then I think what I really "should" be doing is taking some "me" time and exercising regularly so I have more energy to stay on top of everything. And that gets me thinking that I "should" also plan meals and a grocery list each week so that my family and I are eating healthier, too.

Finally, as I was going through my litany of shoulds one day, I realized that I wanted to stop using the word should. It's just too easy to make myself completely miserable over that one little word. If you think about it, who died and decided all these things "should" happen? Who is that Queen of Schedules, Housecleaning and Exercise that decides when and how things should get done? I realized that if I'm always worrying about what "should" happen, I'm not thinking about what IS happening. And the reality is that when I'm not shoulding all over myself, life is pretty darn good.

Sara, Mom of two and graphic designer

---

2. Perfectionism

Hello. My name is Kelly Pryde and I am a recovering perfectionist. Oh wait . . . scratch that. Hello! My name is Kelly Pryde; I'm a recovering perfectionist. No . . . wait . . . still not right . . .

Okay, so "recovering" is the key word in that statement. Yes, I have perfectionist tendencies and I know I'm not the only one! Perfectionism—the unhealthy pursuit of ideal (and sometimes impossible) standards—is another common self-defeating practice amongst us Moms and it rears its ugly head in many ways, shapes, and forms. From obsessing over appearances of our homes, our children, and/or ourselves to striving for success and "the best" in our careers and for our children, and from controlling our emotions so we always appear composed and upbeat to being consumed with doing all the right things as parents, there are many ways we create this kind of emotional clutter for ourselves. And regardless of the perfectionist tendencies Moms may have, the emotional clutter is always the same: stress, anger, worry, frustration, sadness, and a whole lot of guilt. There's nothing perfect about that.

Take a few minutes to consider any perfectionist tendencies you have. Do you spend excessive amounts of time and/or money decorating, remodeling, cleaning, and/or organizing your home? Do you sign your children up for extra activities and buy certain products to help them be "their best"? Have you ever caught yourself doing your child's school project to take it from "good to great"? Are you hung up on reading expert opinions and advice on parenting? Do you become self-critical and guilt-ridden when you make a mistake or fall short of your expectations, either as a parent or in other areas of life?

Whatever type(s) of perfectionism you might have, the root of all perfectionist thinking and behavior comes from the same place. It all stems from a deep-seated belief, a fear that says: "I'm not good enough." Think about that for a moment. Consider the perfectionist tendencies you have and you'll realize that they all link back to that one misguided belief.

Because we have this unconscious idea—this fear—guiding our actions, we set impossible standards and expectations for ourselves. We spend our days trying to do everything we think we should be doing, worrying about what other people think, making sure everything is just right, all with the idea that if everything on the outside is perfect, then we will be okay on the inside.

> **Perfectionism is the voice of the oppressor . . . . It will keep you cramped and insane your whole life.**
> —Anne Lamott

Of course, perfectionists never attain that feeling of "good enough," of being okay. We either run ourselves into the ground from all of the effort perfection requires and we're exhausted. Or we fail to live up to the unrealistic standards we've set for ourselves and we feel depressed and guilty about all the things that don't turn out the way we think they should. Perfectionism keeps us stuck in the world of "never enough," always striving for something more.

And here's the worst part about perfectionism: When we're consumed with striving for that something more and better and best, we lose sight of what's really important in our lives. We don't connect with our partners and children as deeply, we don't see or hear what they really need, and we end up acting out of fear of failure rather than unconditional love.

The reality is that you are okay. There is not one ounce of your being that is not okay. Sure you have some vulnerabilities and things you'd like to improve upon. Who doesn't?! Those vulnerabilities are what make us human and they can be our greatest opportunities for personal growth and acceptance. When you can recognize and embrace those shortcomings rather than hide them under the veil of perfection, when you can accept and appreciate what "is" rather than what "should be," you then begin to make choices that are motivated by love rather than fear, you develop a stronger sense of Self, and you find a more joyful way of being in the world.

Remember that inherent in all perfectionist tendencies is the message of "not good enough." Not only do we feed this message to our bodies, minds, and souls, but our children will also pick up on it—they will learn that message and they will internalize it for themselves. If you choose the message of love and acceptance rather than fear and perfection, you'll be doing yourself, your family, and your children's family a world of good.

FENG SHUI SOLUTIONS FOR PERFECTIONISM

- **Replace judgment and criticism with acceptance and kindness.** Perfectionists tend to be very judgmental and self-critical, especially when they make mistakes. It's that left brain chatter run amok. You can transform those tendencies by "stepping to the right" and speaking to yourself the same way you would to your child—in a gentle, loving way. Find things you are doing well, pat yourself on the back for something—even little things like teaching your child something new, effectively dealing with the drama and attitude of your tween, or simply for making it through the day. Focusing on the things you're doing well and letting go of judgment is an important step towards releasing the emotional clutter of perfectionism.

- **Re-focus your intentions.** When you catch yourself in a perfectionist tendency, ask yourself: "Why am I obsessing over this? Am I doing this out of love or fear of not being/ looking good enough?" Are you really ironing the bed sheets out of love?! Are you really putting the finishing touches on your child's school project because you love him?! Shifting your focus to a more realistic and loving intention and letting go of things that don't serve that intention will alleviate a lot of stress and pressure from both you and your family.

- **Toss "what's best" to the curb and focus on "what matters" instead.** Just like "shoulds" and "have tos," focusing on what's "best" does not serve our mission as Moms and women. It sets us up with unrealistic expectations for our lives and the lives of our children, leading to unnecessary emotional clutter—worry, guilt, and fear. Rather than measure your life against external standards of what's "best," consider your life from the perspective of what really matters to you. You have the best job, but does it allow you to be there for your children when they need you? You have a picture-perfect home, but is it a reflection of who you really are? Does it provide

> **Perfection leaves so little room for mistakes. So little space for acceptance—or joy.**
> —SARAH BAN BREATHNACH

warmth, comfort, and a soft place for your family to fall? You take care of all the little nuances and details in the things you do, but do you have your sanity? Your sanity, your joy, and the little things that matter are far more important than any perfection you seek.

- **Remember this: "What other people think of you is none of your business."** Perfectionists tend to worry a lot about how they appear to others and what other people think of them. What other people think about you, your family, or your parenting is their concern, not yours. If someone wants to pass judgment on you, that's a reflection of that person and his or her character. It doesn't say or change anything about you. Focus on what feels right to you in your heart and you can't go wrong.

What's Draining You?

AVOIDING EXTERNAL SOURCES OF EMOTIONAL CLUTTER

There are several sources of clutter in our external environment that, if left unattended, can also become an enormous drain on our emotional energy. Here are some examples that may be in need of attention in your life . . .

- **Physical Clutter:** Piles of paperwork, stacks of bills, disorganized spaces, baskets of laundry, and unwanted items can be a constant source of energy leakage. Cleaning up and clearing out this kind of clutter is like a breath of fresh air for your emotional energy.
- **TV and Media:** Images and descriptions of negative events create a sense of fear and anxiety in and around us. Be mindful of when and how often you and your family are exposed to this kind of energy—especially first thing in the morning and before bed.
- **Crazymakers:** This is writer Julia Cameron's term for people who create drama, blame, stress, and anxiety in your life and can wreak havoc on your emotional energy. Unfortunately, crazymakers can be your boss, parent, ex, friend, or co-worker. As difficult as it may be, it's important to plug this drain by ending the relationship or establishing clear and firm boundaries with this person.

Following her left brain stroke and recovery, Jill Bolte Taylor keeps a sign in her office that says: "Take responsibility for the energy you bring into this space." Love it. If we each take responsibility for the energy we allow in and around our space, we create a better emotional environment for all of us.

3. Übermom Syndrome

While our own mothers were Supermoms raising us in the latter part of the twentieth century, Moms today have taken that ambition and tenacity to a whole new level. All of our talent and drive combined with the sheer volume of information and products that we contend with everyday and the 24/7 nature of our lives has led to a generation of Übermoms. We have come to believe and live by the maxim: "I can do it all." We not only juggle careers and motherhood, we head up companies, coach little league, and run for office. We are well-versed in organic food, childhood illnesses, and baby sign language. And we Facebook and Twitter about everything from dinner parties to potty training. Yes, we really can do it all. The question is: Do we really *want* to do it all?

Just like our own mothers back in their day, we too are striving. We're striving to be great mothers, great partners, great homemakers, great workers, and happy women. We're striving to be all things to all people all the time, worrying that we are doing enough and that we will *be* enough. And it's too much. All the running around, all the striving to get it all done, wears us down and keeps us stuck in worry, fear, and guilt. It's time to walk Übermom, and Supermom, Wondermom, and every other "mom," to the curb.

> **We're trying to be everything all the time. The best mom, the best worker, the best wife . . . and it's too much.**
> —TERI HATCHER

Of course, Übermom Syndrome has a lot to do with our culture and socialization as well as our biological instinct to tend (remember the tending instinct—our stress response to look after others at all costs—we discussed earlier?). But at the end of the day, it really comes down to how each of us thinks about this need to run around at Mach 10 in order to get everything done. For example, do you have a chronic need to please other people, including your children, afraid they won't like you if you say "no"? Do you have trouble asking for help, worried what other people might think about your ability to handle things or that you might inconvenience them? Or do you believe that all this doing is necessary in order to be successful? Once we are able to identify the fears and worries—the emotional clutter—that underlie our übermom tendencies, we can begin to change our minds about how we go about our days as Moms and women and we can clear the way for a calmer, more joyful way of being.

In my own life and in my work with other Moms, I have found that there are three main areas where we tend to get stuck in Übermom Syndrome: 1) people-pleasing and the inability to say "no;" 2) asking for and accepting help; and 3) over-achieving. Let's take a closer look at each of these types of clutter and some solutions for clearing them out.

FENG SHUI SOLUTIONS FOR ÜBERMOM SYNDROME

- **Learning how to say "no."** I have worked with so many Moms who do too much simply because they can't say "no." They are overextended, have trouble setting limits with their children, and they are tired, yet they continue to say yes to demands on their time and energy. They say yes when they really want to say no and end up stressed out, resentful, and running on empty as a result. Why do we do this to ourselves? What is so hard about saying no?

For most of us, saying no stems from insecurities and fears about what other people might think of us if we say no. While on the surface we may think we're doing the right thing by giving and helping others whenever we can, deep down we're really afraid that people will think less of us if we say no. We worry that our kids will say we're mean and stop speaking to us if we don't give them what they ask for. We worry that our husband's friends will think we're a b**ch for saying no to one more guys' weekend. Deep down all the yeses really just stem from a need to be loved and accepted.

> Half of the troubles of this life can be traced to saying yes too quickly and not saying no soon enough.
>
> —Josh Billings

But here's the thing: Doing things that you don't genuinely want to do for another person is a very unloving thing to do—to yourself and to others. Betraying your own needs and desires and your own sense of what feels right to gain someone else's approval does not benefit anyone. It merely creates unhealthy emotional clutter in your life and your relationships. When you realize that saying no is an important step in protecting your emotional energy—an energy that affects you and everyone around you—it becomes much easier to say this small but powerful word.

In the event that saying no feels like a very daunting task for you, here are a few tips to get you started:

1. *The first no is always the hardest.* Saying no gets easier with time once you realize that turning down a request or demand will not result in your collapse as a human being! In fact, you'll feel a whole new sense of freedom and respect when you begin to stand up for your emotional energy and your sense of what feels right for you.

2. *"No." is a complete sentence.* In many cases, we say yes to requests merely because we can't think of a reason or an excuse to say no. But saying no doesn't require a lengthy excuse or explanation. We can simply say "no" and leave it at that. This is one of the best pieces of advice I've ever received and it has become second nature to me now.

While it does feels strange to say no and not follow it up with anything (in fact, most people will look at you in silence waiting for your follow-up to the no), giving a simple no is perfectly acceptable. Many women choose to extend this statement slightly to "No, thank you" just to add a politeness factor. One group of Moms I worked with even decided to use the excuse that they were "protecting their emotional energy" when approached with a request they were struggling to say no to. Prepare a no statement that works for you and use it as needed.

3. *Remember this age-old wisdom:* Dr. Seuss used to say "*The people who matter don't mind, and the people who mind don't matter.*" This couldn't be truer than when it comes to saying no to someone. The people in your life who truly love and care about you will understand and respect your no. End of story. Well, okay, maybe that doesn't apply to our children! They'll likely be upset and have a few choice words for us regardless. But then, that's all part and parcel of being a parent. We're certainly not in a popularity contest when it comes to doing what's right for our children's emotional and physical well-being. Even though they can't articulate it yet, they will respect us and benefit a whole lot more when we set firm and loving boundaries for them. And in then end, isn't that what really matters?

- **Help is not a four letter word!** Just like saying no, asking for and accepting help is another prickly topic for many Moms. Most of us don't reach out and ask for help because we don't want people to think we can't handle things and/or because we don't want to inconvenience anyone. Sometimes we're so far gone running on empty that we don't even know what we need. And sometimes we feel like others won't do things the "right" way, so we just do it all ourselves. All that to say, a whole lot of emotional clutter—fear, worry, stress, and pride—gets in the way of us reaching out to others for help. Then of course, we add to that clutter by running around at Mach 10 doing everything ourselves.

The truth is that as much as we're culturalized to be strong and independent members of society, we are naturally dependent on one another in many ways, too. It's called a support system and humans have been creating them since the beginning of time in order to survive. While today's isolated nuclear families and strong values on independence make it difficult for Moms to ask for help, it is a critical skill for us to master if we are to protect our emotional energy and be the Moms and women we want to be.

> **Nobody before has ever asked the nuclear family to live all by itself in a box the way we do. With no relatives, no support, we've put it in an impossible situation.**
>
> —Margaret Mead

Here are some ideas to consider for clearing out the emotional clutter that gets in our way of asking for and accepting help:

1. *Know and embrace your support system.* There is a lot of wisdom in the proverb that says "It takes a village to raise a child." While many of us don't have the support system of an extended family within arms reach these days, it's important to identify your network of family, friends, and neighbors who will be there to provide you with unconditional support when needed. Your "village" does not have to consist of a multitude of people. A mother or sister to call when you're having a bad day, a neighbor to call in a pinch, a friend who can bring a casserole for dinner when you're sick, and even your partner who can allow you to take an uninterrupted shower is all the village you need. Remember that Mom is only one person—something I remind my kids all the time. Know your limit and stay within it by reaching out to your village when you need it. And when someone in your village extends a helping hand to you, accept it with an open mind and a gracious heart knowing that you are blessed with people who care about you.

2. *Don't wait for a crisis situation to ask for help.* Recognizing the warning signs of Übermom Syndrome and running on empty is key to staying within your limits of functionality and well-being. All too often Moms keep doing and doing until they find themselves at the breaking point. When that happens, rational thought and common sense are out the window and it's very difficult to formulate and articulate your thoughts on what you need help with. (Not to mention you may be a raving lunatic by that point scaring potential helpers away!) Again, knowing your personal limits on what you can manage and asking for help before you reach those limits will go a long way in curbing your übermom tendencies.

3. *Just ask . . . and be specific about what you need.* Most Moms and women are very intuitive about sensing when another person needs help. In those times, we either offer our help or jump in and do what needs to be done. But not everyone in our immediate environment is that tuned in and intuitive to sense when us Moms need help. For this reason, it's important to speak up and ask for what you need. Don't wait for your husband or kids or friend to notice that you're struggling and need help. You could be waiting an awfully long time for assistance while you sink further and further into emotional clutter. Before you reach running on empty crisis mode, calmly and

> **Men need rule books. Women want men to intuit what they want. Only 2% of men can do that, and most of them are not heterosexual.**
>
> —Dennis Prager

clearly articulate what exactly you need and work with your friend or loved one to get the help you're looking for.

4. *Check your ego at the door.* Once you've asked for help it's important to let go of unrealistic standards or expectations for how that help shows up. No, not everyone is going to get things done the way you do them—your husband will not buy the organic orange juice you buy, your mother-in-law will not feed your kids the sugar-free cereal you do, and your kids will not tidy their rooms and make their beds the way you do. Let it go! Your clutter-free emotional energy is far more important than the minute details that don't mean anything in the grand scheme of things.

Lastly, remember that asking for and accepting help is not an admission of failure or lack of competence. Wise Moms ask for help not because they can't do something themselves, but because they want to have the emotional energy to be the Moms and women they're meant to be. Period.

- **Keep your ambition in check.** A large part of Übermom Syndrome and running on empty stems from drive, ambition, and over-achievement. This is not surprising given the culture we live in. We spend years achieving in school and college/university then we embark on careers and strive to climb that ladder of success. When our children are born, we want to be successful parents too, and we make every effort to learn and do all the right things for them so that they can be their best. It's that go-getter left brain run amok that keeps us stuck in worry, competition, and constant doing.

While we'll explore this topic in much more detail in Path Six when we rethink balance and priorities, for now it's helpful to consider two approaches to keeping our ambition in check: *perspective* and *patience*. *Perspective* simply means that we can step back long enough to look at the bigger picture of our lives and ask ourselves questions like: "Do I like what I see?" "Am I happy?" "Am I focusing on what *really* matters to me?" "Why am I doing X, and Y and Z? Am I doing these things out of fear and competition or love and meaning?" "What would happen if I stopped doing X, Y and/or Z?" When we can answer these questions honestly and shift from thoughts and behaviors that stem from fear, worry, and stress to thoughts and behaviors grounded in love and meaning, we clear out a lot of emotional clutter. That's when we can walk Übermom confidently to the curb.

> I think there's an ongoing effort involved in trying to get a bigger perspective, trying to let go of things that limit your capacity to love.
>
> —MEG RYAN

Keeping our ambition in check doesn't mean we give up on our dreams or stop setting goals for ourselves. It means that we learn the fine art of *patience* and stop trying to do it all and be it all and have it all at one time. Rose Kennedy used to say that life is a marathon, not a sprint. There is a lot of wisdom in that philosophy for us as Moms. If we try to sprint our way through motherhood with all of our striving and doing, we will miss out on so many wonderful moments and opportunities during the small window of time our children are home with us. So the laundry doesn't get folded and the dirty dishes stay in the sink overnight. So the corner office is not yours in six months and you have to wait another year to remodel your kitchen. So your child only signs up for one activity instead of three. Does it really matter if putting these things off means you and your family will have more calm, connection, and sanity in the meantime? Patience allows us to step away from the über-stress and über-worry about what will be and sink into the simple comfort and happiness of what is.

Reinvention Practice

HONORING YOUR PERSONAL ENERGY TYPE

Knowing your personal energy type is also important for understanding and respecting your emotional energy needs and limitations as a Mom. According to psychological theory, there are two ways people get personal energy: by engaging in the outer world of people and activities (the extrovert or "outie" type) or by engaging in their inner world of ideas and experiences (the introvert or "innie" type). Here's how they differ:

Outies get their energy by being with other people and by engaging in lots of activity. When outies have time alone or don't have the opportunity to interact with others, they can get quite irritable and restless. For Moms who are outies, this translates into challenges being isolated at home with their children. As much as you love being with them, you need more stimulation and interaction. Be sure to go on outings with other Moms, chat on the phone with a friend when you can, or plan a night out with friends so you can re-energize.

Innies benefit from reflecting on thoughts and ideas and need time alone to recharge their batteries. Too many external demands and a lot of social interaction can overwhelm innies and drain their energy. For Moms, this type becomes easily drained from the high energy demands of motherhood, a career, and all the social activity that comes with these roles. Let your family know that you need space and find alone time where you can recharge. Go for a walk, take fifteen minutes for a cup of tea before picking up your kids from school, or have a bubble bath—even if it means you're eating cereal for dinner!

To identify your personal energy type, you can complete the quiz at the back of the book in Appendix A. Once you know your type, you will be able to replenish your energy more readily, you'll feel far less guilty about your needs, and you'll have more energy for the things that matter most.

---

4. Stuck in Pissosity

Pissosity is what happens when we get stuck in frustration, anger, and resentment. We've all been in this clutter zone at one time or another and we all know it ain't pretty. Moms who get stuck in pissosity display a number of characteristic behaviors:

- *Complaining* about everything from being tired, to nobody helping out, to things being unfair, to nobody looking after her needs.
- *Judging and criticizing* the way the neighbor disciplines her kids, the cereal Dad buys, the way the kids make their beds, the TV shows Grandma lets the kids watch.
- *Blaming* everyone else for why she's tired, unhappy, and in a bad mood.

> **If you are irritated by every rub, how will you ever be polished?**
>
> —RUMI

Of course, some of our pissosity can be related to hormonal shifts at certain times of the month. These bouts are temporary and tend to pass relatively quickly. In fact, renowned neuropsychiatrist Daniel Amen suggests eating some high carb "mood foods" such as bread, pasta, or chocolate for a quick boost in serotonin to resolve these kinds of temporary hormonal shifts. But there are also many times when we get stuck in these tendencies for extended periods because of our cluttered thoughts and attitudes and the fact that we're running on empty. And unfortunately, when we're stuck in the pool of pissosity, we drag everyone around us down into it, too.

Remember that anger in and of itself is not a negative thing. It's when we get stuck there and ruminate in bitter, resentful thoughts that anger becomes one of the most toxic, unhealthy emotions in the human body and in our relationships. Anger is meant to propel us into action to change what it is we don't like. And if we can't change it, then anger can teach us how to change our thoughts and find ways to accept the situation. Here's how:

FENG SHUI SOLUTIONS FOR STUCK IN PISSOSITY

- **Choose flight over fight.** Anger builds upon anger. This is how emotional clutter builds up in our minds and bodies—frustration leads to irritability, irritability to anger, and anger to rage and resentment. It is literally a series of chemical releases that build on one another to ready our bodies for fight or flight. For this reason, it's important to nip anger in the bud and deal with feelings of frustration before they fester and shift us into pissosity. Distracting ourselves with a "time-out" is a very powerful cooling down technique that can diffuse frustration and anger—it's the same approach we use with our little ones. Taking a walk, calling a friend, heading to a local café to write in your journal, and even locking yourself in the bathroom to recite a song or prayer can do wonders for distracting our minds from thoughts of pissosity.

In her book, *My Stroke of Insight*, neuroscientist Jill Bolte Taylor explains that the process in the brain that triggers our anger and readies us for fight or flight only lasts about ninety seconds. Ninety seconds!! Any anger that lingers beyond that is by choice. We stay in a state of pissosity because we've chosen to hang on to angry thoughts and feelings. So training ourselves to stop, breathe, and change our minds through distraction during those ninety seconds will go a long way in shifting out of anger and frustration. (Remember the breathing practice "Waiting to Inhale" in Path One? Also see "The Patience Plan" reinvention practice later in this chapter for ideas on calming the mind.)

The Mommy Diaries

MY AHA MOMENT: EMBRACING CHAOS

Picture this: I'm scrambling to make dinner one evening, the kids are hungry and cranky, my husband has just come home from work and is trying to tell me about his day, my daughter is crying—she's trying to do a puzzle and "no one EVER helps her," my son is hanging off my leg, and the chicken is way overdone. Sound familiar?!

Normally I'd have a mini meltdown at this point and tell everyone to freeze because "Mom can't think with all the racket!" But for some reason this particular evening, I reacted to the chaos in a completely unexpected way. Rather than lose my cool, I felt an unusual calmness and smiled as I thought to myself: "This is being a family." It was an Aha moment.

I realized that chaos—all the hurriedness, tantrums, squabbles, and annoyances—are actually signs of a normal, healthy family. And in truth, it was my negative view of the chaos that led all of it to wear on my nerves and rob me of my energy. It had become all too automatic for me to get irritated and react with: "I can't handle this" and "I'm losing it here!"

As I began to embrace chaos, I found myself dealing with things more calmly and rationally and being a more loving, tolerant person—qualities that I know will serve my children well as they go out into the world. And while embracing chaos doesn't mean I don't lose my temper or that things don't fall apart (because there are still plenty of those times!), I continue to remind myself that patience is always just a thought away.

Kelly Pryde, Mom of two and parent coach

- **Let go of hang-ups on fairness.** "It's not fair" is the battle cry of many a Mom stuck in pissosity. We complain because we do all the tidying and housework, organize all the activities and appointments, and plan all the meals and groceries. We get irritated that we play dress-up and listen to Barney all day with our little one while Dad's idea of one-on-one time is sitting on the sofa watching football together. We change more diapers, we do more tuck-ins, we do more bath times. And it's not fair! Nope, it probably isn't. But then nobody ever said that life is fair—birds eat worms, floods destroy homes, magnolia blooms only last a week . . . and mothers are primary caregivers. The natural order of things may not always seem fair, but it is *what is* and walking around being angry about it, scrumbling about it, and complaining about it won't change a thing. The only thing we can change is how we think about it and how we react to it. Irritated about doing all the tidying? Enlist your family to help. Frustrated about doing all the groceries? Make a list and kindly ask Dad to take the kids out to get them once in a while. Angry about Dad's way of spending time with the kids? Let Dad do things differently. Remember that Moms and Dads are not created equal—we are meant to complement rather than replicate one another. Be flexible and willing to accept the things Dad does in his unique way. And when there are legitimate issues . . .

- **Communicate your feelings before they fester.** If something is bothering you, TALK ABOUT IT! Don't wait until you're in a full blown state of pissosity when your rational mind has been emotionally highjacked and you've lost it. Discuss your feelings long before that point or well after

> Try to communicate your thoughts and feelings IN THE MOMENT THAT IT'S HAPPENING with grace and understanding, so it doesn't linger like old broccoli in the fridge. That stinks!
> —RITA WILSON

you've cooled down. How often have you stomped around complaining about things and scrumbling in your mind about something you don't like? Then when your husband or children ask you what's wrong you bark, "Nothing!" and get even angrier because they actually had to ask what's bothering you. Can't they see what's wrong? Sheesh. Remember that Moms are wired to intuit what's wrong; the rest of our family is not. For this reason, we need to tell them what's on our mind—in a cool, collected way—otherwise the clutter builds up and creates a lot of what I call "bad mojo" in our minds, bodies, homes, and relationships. Living with bad mojo is not good for anybody. Let people know what's bothering you, what your needs are, and work towards a solution together.

- **Surrender and forgive.** *A Course in Miracles* says, "You are never angry for the reason you think." This is so true. If we continue to find ourselves stuck in pissosity, there is likely a deeper issue triggering that anger: issues from childhood, a marital grievance, a wronged relationship, or some other injustice that has left us wounded. We all have them. If we fail to heal these wounds, the anger and hurt we hold onto gradually turns into bitterness and resentment towards the person who wronged us. These stuffed emotions can not only affect our health as we saw in "The Anatomy of Emotional Dis-Ease" section earlier in this chapter, but also our relationships as they often translate into criticism, blame, jealousy, and even cynicism.

An honest and deep inquiry into our feelings will often reveal the real roots of our pissosity. For most of us, that can be done through quiet space, reflection, and journaling. For others who have suffered deeper wounds through abuse or trauma, some form of counseling or therapy may be necessary. Once we've identified the root of our anger, we can release the bitterness and resentment by forgiving the person who has wronged us.

Contrary to what many people believe, forgiveness is not about condoning what the other person did. It actually has very little to do with the other person. Forgiveness is simply the act of giving something up. We give up our need to hold on to the anger and blame that we think is punishing the person who wronged us. We let go of hurt that we think we need to hold onto because it's part of who we are. In reality, all of that anger and bitterness is merely "friendly fire"—it's an attack on our selves and our loved ones. When we recognize that prolonged anger and hurt doesn't serve a purpose—it won't punish the person you're angry with, it won't change anything, and it has nothing to do with who we are—we can start to let it go. We can think about the person who wronged us and know that they did the best they could do at the time, even if it was really lousy. We can set healthy boundaries to protect ourselves from someone who continues to wrong us by walking away, maintaining distance, or

> Forgiveness is the fragrance the violet sheds on the heel that has crushed it.
> —Mark Twain

standing up for ourselves. We can tell ourselves that we are choosing love and compassion over anger and resentment, for our own good and the good of our loved ones who share our lives with us. This is how we begin to heal past hurts and open the parts of our heart that have been closed off for so long. Forgiveness allows us to awaken a joy in ourselves that has long been forgotten.

Khaled Hosseini describes forgiveness beautifully in his book, *The Kite Runner,* when he says, "I wondered if that was how forgiveness budded, not with the fanfare of epiphany, but with pain gathering its things, packing up, and slipping away unannounced in the middle of the night." This is true for most people when they choose forgiveness—you likely won't experience an epiphany or huge emotional release, but you'll know forgiveness is flourishing when you think about the person who wronged you and there is no sting or bitterness associated with the thought. All the hurt and angry clutter just quietly disappears.

Reinvention Practice

THE UNSENT LETTER: FORGIVING, HEALING, AND MOVING ON

Because forgiveness is something we do for ourselves, we don't have to have an actual conversation with someone to forgive them. A powerful way to forgive someone and move on is to write them an "unsent letter."

An unsent letter involves expressing all of your hurt and anger to the person who has wronged you without ever actually sending it. Although it helps to start with "Dear _____"etiquette is not required for this letter. Simply write about whatever comes to mind when you imagine that you are telling this person why you are angry, hurt, and disappointed. Imagine that he or she is listening and let everything out without worrying about censorship, language, or grammar. In the end, this letter is for your eyes only.

Pouring out unexpressed feelings will be a very emotional issue, so it's important to find the time and space for this exercise. Once you have expressed everything—what happened, how you felt (e.g., unloved, abandoned, betrayed, unimportant, etc), and what you believed about yourself—write about what you have learned. What do you realize now as an adult? What beliefs do you *know* are no longer true? How has this wrong made you grow as a person? How do you see this person differently now? Acknowledge and accept what you have learned and forgive him or her.

Some people find it helpful to go one step further and write themselves a return letter from the person they were angry with. For this letter, you write to yourself as the other person imagining what he or she would say if they were emotionally healed and whole. How would that person explain his or her past behavior and apologize to you? This is a way of making amends with that person in your heart so that you can further your healing and move on.

---

5. Something More

In her classic memoir, *Gift from the Sea*, Anne Morrow Lindbergh shares her insights on motherhood in 1950s American culture. Even though her words were written over half a century ago, they still hold true for many running on empty mothers in our culture today. Lindbergh writes, "I believe that what woman resents is not so much giving herself in pieces as giving herself purposelessly. What we fear is not so much that our energy may be leaking through small outlets as that it may be going 'down the drain.'" I've felt this and many of the Moms I work with feel it. That nagging sense as we change diapers, feed our families, manage our homes, run errands, and juggle relationships, working day in and day out, that there must be something more. A certain sadness and hopelessness leads us to ask "Is this all there is?"

Rather than sit and reflect on this sadness and what might be missing in our lives, most Moms either wallow in the depressed feelings becoming resentful, lonely, and emotionally drained or they stuff the feelings away by keeping busy and filling the void with more clutter—clothes, home décor, knowledge, food, or substances. Our tendency is to resist these feelings and look for a way out because we view them as dark, empty, and unknown. But we can think about sadness and depression as more than negative feelings needing treatment or "numbing." We can view them as a natural part of the life cycle that signals a need for isolation, a need to empty our plates and just be quiet for some time. And if we just take the time to sit and be with the sadness for awhile, we will often find valuable information about what's really missing in our lives.

> **Sure I get depressed. But I never feel like it's a bad thing. That's part of the journey in life and if you have to go there, you go there.**
> —KATE HUDSON

Now, I'm not suggesting that Moms embrace and sit with this kind of depression and sadness for weeks at a time. That would not be helpful or healthy for anyone. But if we can sit with these feelings mindfully for a brief time, we usually discover that what's missing in our lives is *connection*— connection to Self, connection to our children, partner, or loved ones and/or connection to life itself. Once we make this discovery, we can begin to make the connections that add the meaning and purpose that is often the "something more" that is missing for many of us.

Here are some ways we can begin making the connections to that something more:

FENG SHUI SOLUTIONS FOR SOMETHING MORE

1. **Step to the right into feeling.** When darker feelings of sadness and depression creep in, try acknowledging them rather than resisting or wallowing in them. Consider what it is you have lost or feel is missing from your life. Try not to judge the feelings by letting anger and thoughts of unfairness creep in or by allowing discouragement and hopelessness to take over. Know that this is temporary. Simply feel the sadness and try to identify what's missing for you: loss of freedom, loss of purpose, loss of self, loss of intimacy. Finding quiet space to reflect or write in a journal will help you get in touch with these feelings.

2. **Make the connection.** Once you've identified what is missing, think about ways you can begin to re-connect with what is lost. Are you missing YOU? What are some little things you can do just for yourself? (Note: We'll discuss YOU further on the next pathway.) Are you lonely and missing an intimate connection with your partner? Plan a date for just the two of you, even if it's a quiet dinner at home after the kids go to bed. Commit to hugging each other more often. Are you tired of the monotony of your daily routine? Be creative and do something different—have a pancake breakfast for dinner or sneak out to a movie one afternoon. Is your work lacking meaning and fulfillment? What steps can you take to begin finding the purpose you seek? Is it time for a new role or a career change? Do you have a passion that is waiting to be expressed? Sometimes our something more leads us to bigger life questions and decisions and sometimes it leads us to the little things that are right in front of us everyday. We'll explore this topic further over the next two chapters, but for now simply taking the time to consider our something more and making small connections is the first step towards more joy and fulfillment.

3. **Embrace change.** Sometimes sadness and depression signals a new season of life that we must move through rather than resist or try to change. Throughout our lives as Moms and women we continue to go through stages of development and relationships. The transition to motherhood is by far one of the biggest leaps to a new stage of life as our relationships, demands, priorities, and skill requirements

> **Hiding the dark places results in a loss of soul; speaking for them and from them offers a way toward genuine community and intimacy.**
>
> —THOMAS MOORE

change dramatically. Feelings of depression during this time can indicate that we are trying to hold on to what we once knew and were comfortable with or to what we think *should be*. This, too, is a lack of connection as we become disconnected from life as it is.

As we will explore in Path Six on the art of letting go, the natural process of life is not something we can control—it unfolds and flows in its own way with both highs and lows. Trusting in this process and connecting to life in this way—with its highs and lows, knowns and unknowns—allows us to develop not only the sense of having lived through something and of being older and wiser, but also of acceptance and patience for what is at any given moment of our lives. As inspirational author Iyanla Vanzant often says, "Wherever you are is exactly where you're supposed to be." Embrace that and open yourself up to the wisdom and growth that is available to you during the challenging times you encounter.

* * * * *

The thirteenth-century mystical poet, Rumi, wrote a wonderful poem called *The Guest House* which offers us timeless wisdom for managing our emotional house as we journey through life and motherhood:

This being human is a guest house.
Every morning a new arrival.

A joy, a depression, a meanness,
some momentary awareness comes
as an unexpected visitor.

Welcome and entertain them all!
Even if they are a crowd of sorrows,
who violently sweep your house
empty of its furniture,
still, treat each guest honorably.
He may be clearing you out
for some new delight.

The dark thought, the shame, the malice.
Meet them at the door laughing and invite them in.

Be grateful for whatever comes.
Because each has been sent
as a guide from beyond.

Welcome your feeling guests into your emotional house. Listen and learn from them as you accept what they have to offer, even if you don't particularly care for or understand them at the time. Do not obsess or dote over them and do not let them overstay their welcome—there is nothing gracious about that. Once you've spent time with your guests and heeded their guidance, let them be on their way. Then, move on.

REFLECTION AND ACTION FOR PATH THREE

- Which emotional clutter zone(s) is most prominent for you as a Mom? What thoughts and practices do you have that contribute to that clutter and drain your emotional energy? What one feng shui solution or reinvention practice can you commit to today to begin clearing it out?

- Louise Hay, pioneer of the self-help movement and author of *You Can Heal Your Life,* believes that much of our emotional clutter stems from a lack of forgiveness. Where are you withholding forgiveness in your life? When you think about the people in your life, both past and present, who brings up feelings of bitterness or resentment for you? You might try the forgiveness practice ("The Unsent Letter") to begin the processing of clearing out the emotional clutter in this area of your life.

- Are you your own best friend or your own worst enemy? To be the Moms and women we're meant to be, it is essential that we are our own best friends. How can you speak to yourself more kindly? Where can you forgive yourself and be more supportive for mistakes you have made? How can you take care of yourself in more loving ways? A worst enemy will drag you down to low, stagnant levels of energy (or "bad mojo"), whereas, a best friend will raise you up to levels of higher, more vibrant energy. Choose wisely.

FURTHER READING FOR PATH THREE

Anatomy of the Spirit by Caroline Myss (New York: Three Rivers Press, 1996)

Acclaimed medical intuitive Caroline Myss presents a breakthrough model of how emotional issues, psychological stresses, and beliefs affect specific areas of the body to create illness. A must-read for understanding the mind-body-spirit connection.

Your Erroneous Zones by Wayne W. Dyer, Ph.D. (New York: Avon Books, 1995)

Originally written in 1976, this classic is one of the top selling books of all time, having sold over 35 million copies. It instructs readers on how to escape negative, self-defeating thinking and take charge of their emotional well-being.

The Emotional Energy Factor by Mira Kirshenbaum (New York: Bantam Dell, 2003)

A psychotherapist and researcher offers 25 easy-to-read, practical strategies for increasing emotional energy and adding more joy and vitality to life.

The Feeling Good Handbook by David D. Burns, M.D. (New York: Plume, 1999)

A bestselling author and psychiatrist offers clear and easy-to-use guidelines, examples, and exercises for dealing with fear, anxiety, depression, interpersonal difficulties and other types of self-defeating thinking. It's like a cognitive therapy session in a book!

PATH 4

YOU, YOURSELF AND YOU

Rediscovering the You That's Not "Mom"

It doesn't interest me what you do for a living.
I want to know what you ache for
and if you dare to dream of meeting your heart's longing.

. . . .

It doesn't interest me
to know where you live or how much money you have.
I want to know if you can get up
after the night of grief and despair
weary and bruised to the bone
and do what needs to be done
to feed the children.

It doesn't interest me who you know
or how you came to be here.
I want to know if you will stand
in the center of the fire
with me
and not shrink back.

It doesn't interest me where or what or with whom
you have studied.
I want to know what sustains you

> *from the inside*
> *when all else falls away.*
>
> *I want to know if you can be alone*
> *with yourself*
> *and if you truly like the company you keep*
> *in the empty moments.*

—ORIAH MOUNTAIN DREAMER, *The Invitation*

Do you know who you are? I mean really know who YOU are, beyond your biography and all of the roles that you play. Mom, wife, daughter, sister, career woman, volunteer—these are all of the characteristics by which we tend to define ourselves. They are the labels that make up our biographical "you." "I'm thirty-five years old and a divorced mother of three," "I'm a stay-at-home mom," "I'm a wife, mother of two, and part-time law clerk," "I'm Johnny's mom." With all of the roles we play as Moms and women, it's no wonder so many of us lose our personal sense of self.

But what happens when you let all of the labels fall away? Who are you without your biography? If I asked you to tell me about who you are without using any biographical details, what would you say?

What's left when you can't talk about the biographical "you" is the more profound, essential "YOU"—the YOU with all of its passions, uniqueness, and talents, the YOU that doesn't change if you get divorced or lose your job, the YOU that has never before existed in all of time. This is the part of ourselves that we are rarely invited to discover through our education and our careers. It's the part of ourselves that begins to whisper to us in motherhood when we're running on empty because all of our time and energy is focused on our outer roles of mom, wife, daughter, career woman, etc. We become so disconnected from that inner sense of Self—the real person at the heart of all these outer roles—that it begins to remind us that there is something more.

YOU are not your biography. Being a mom does not define who you are. Who YOU are as a unique individual defines the kind of Mom you are. As Moms and women, it is important that we understand this and take steps to reconnect with our inner YOU. Because at the end of the day, we can be doing all the right things and all the best things for our children in all of our various roles, but our doing alone will never be enough if we neglect being. Constant doing that is not rooted in being lacks

> **You're a better parent the more yourself you are. 'You' have to be there. You have to be a 'person' there, not just 'mom'.**
>
> —JULIAN MOORE

joy, meaning, and connection. It lacks real love. In this way, the excavation of and connection with Self is at the heart of reinvention. It is an essential aspect of living and being, not only for our own personal strength and fulfillment, but also for connecting in a meaningful way with others and helping our children develop a strong sense of Self for themselves. If you think about it, our unique Self, our being, is one of the greatest gifts we have to offer our children.

This pathway will guide you on the journey of discovering and embracing the aspects of your Self that you have long disconnected from: your unique qualities, your inner brilliance, and your heart-felt longings. As you reconnect with YOU, decisions and questions about motherhood, parenting, career, love, and life will become much clearer to you and you will begin to live and parent on your own terms with far more confidence, joy, and fulfillment.

THE ART OF BEING SELF-FUL

The first step in reconnecting with your inner Self is to get comfortable with and serious about taking time for yourself. This is a real challenge for many of us. With our myriad of to-dos and commitments, we often think that we don't have time for such a luxury. Many Moms who are accustomed to running around at Mach 10 feel uncomfortable about down time alone with thoughts about "What on earth would I do?" or deeper worries about what they might discover there. And then there are some who feel that taking time for yourself is a selfish thing to do; they feel guilty and believe in the notion that mothers are supposed to be "selfless." So let's set the record straight.

Firstly, time for self is not a luxury. While getting time alone "sans kids" often feels like a luxury, it really is a necessity. Much like brushing our teeth and taking a shower, it is an integral part of our regular hygiene. Go too long without it and a misery of sorts will most certainly set in. In fact, the seventeenth-century philosopher Blaise Pascal once commented that all of our miseries stem from our inability to sit quietly in a room alone. And as many wise mothers who came before us urge: Women need real moments of solitude in order to balance how much of themselves they give away and to find again the true essence of themselves.

> My best advice for a mother would be . . . to make sure you carve out chunks of time—no matter how small they are—for yourself so you can reflect, regroup and re-energize.
>
> —U.S. First Lady Michelle Obama

Secondly, while thoughts of taking time by yourself can be uncomfortable and even daunting for many, this chapter will give you plenty of things to focus on and consider during your alone time. As I mentioned in the first pathway on stepping to the right, taking time for yourself is not about sitting on a mountaintop and chanting for hours at a time. It's about being alone with yourself and getting to truly like the company you keep in those empty moments. I have always found it helpful to consider time alone as time "with my Self" rather than "by myself." If you don't want to be alone with you, why would anyone else?!

Finally, the idea of being "selfless" is just that: it is a state of being that is without self. I don't know about you, but this is certainly not a state that I want for myself or to model for my children. Talk about running on empty. Taking time to care for yourself, connect with your Self, and look after your needs is a very "Self-ful" thing to do. Being Self-ful is how we infuse ourselves and our being into the things we do as Moms and women. And there's nothing self-absorbed or selfish about that.

I know you've heard about the importance of self-care a million times: "You have to put yourself first," "You have to take care of yourself before you can take care of others," etc., etc. (Notice all the tyrannical "have-to's" in those commonly heard statements?) But the art of being Self-ful is much more than self-care. It goes much deeper than going for a manicure or shopping for a new pair of shoes. This leg of the reinvention journey is about building a relationship with YOU. Just like the budding of a close friendship or romantic relationship, it's about digging past all the biographical stuff of the ego self—title, education, income, and possessions, and getting to the heart of the essential Self—what sustains you from the inside when all else falls away.

Like the formation of any new relationship, being Self-ful takes time, effort, inquiry, and intimacy. It requires that you be open and honest with yourself and that you withhold judgment as you explore your passions, talents, and longings. It requires that you ask honest questions, even if you don't like or are afraid of where the answers might lead you. Your new relationship with Self *will* lead to change—some subtle, some dramatic, some short-term and some long-term. But change is inevitable, and natural. Not being honest with ourselves and fighting change is how we betray ourselves. It's like sweeping our hearts and souls under a rug. Discounting your Self will not make the longings and whispers of your heart go away and it certainly won't allow you to become the Mom and woman you're meant to be. It's time to get Self-ful so that you can live more deeply, honestly, and joyfully. The only question that remains is: Are you ready to meet YOU?

The Mommy Diaries

BECOMING THE LEAD IN MY OWN LIFE

Six years into motherhood and I felt like people knew me only as "Jim's wife" or "Michael and Sara's mom." No one knew me just as Cheryl. I felt like I was defined solely by my relationship to other people, like I was a supporting actress in someone else's movie, rather than the lead role in my own life.

Finding myself had nothing to do with getting away, taking a vacation, or being footloose and fancy-free. It was purely about discovering who I was as a unique individual.

For me, the key was finding something that I *loved* and giving myself permission to go do it. Sometimes that simply meant going out for lunch with a friend to talk about things that mattered to us or taking the time to read a book that inspired me. Eventually it meant going back to school to become a teacher. All these things allowed me to be the *ME* that wasn't "mom" or "wife," but that was everything Cheryl.

Cheryl, Mom of two and kindergarten teacher

JOURNEY TO THE CENTER OF THE SELF

In Path One on reclaiming the feminine, I shared the story of my intuition beginning to whisper to me when my graduate supervisor thanked me for my machine-like dedication and productivity. While that incident wasn't a revelationary light-bulb moment, it was definitely a nudge from the Universe saying, "Ahem." It got my attention. So a few months later when I heard a guest on The Oprah Show talking about the inner Self and how to find more joy and meaning in life, I was intrigued. Little did I know this guest would ask the one question that would change my life and set me on the path of reinvention. The question? . . .

What is your heart's desire?

It was such a simple question, yet it hit me like a ton of bricks. *What is your heart's desire?* I didn't have the first damn clue! I had never thought about that before. It had never even occurred to me to think about it, and it scared the bejeebers out of me that I didn't know how to answer a question that seemed like such an important thing to know. But I had only ever been taught to think with my head—to analyze, solve, organize, and plan. And the more I thought about it and reflected on my life at the time, the more I realized that much of my life was purely a reflection of my head. While everything seemed great on the surface, I couldn't help but think that my life just looked really good on paper; it was all biographical stuff. There was no heart.

> Sometime in your life you will go on a journey. It will be the longest journey you have ever taken. It is the journey to find yourself.
>
> —KATHERINE SHARP

This is where my journey began.

As I began to downshift from my head to my heart, more questions began to surface, relevant ideas and people seemed to find me, and synchronicities started to unfold. Although I didn't realize it at the time, a pathway to Self was emerging in front of me. It's the same pathway that we will journey together over the next several pages. Much of what you've already been working on in the previous pathways—stepping into the right mind and becoming mindful of how you feel—has prepared you for this journey. So tune in to your heart and your feelings and walk with me . . .

The Essential YOU

Have you ever met someone and walked away with the impression that you didn't really care much for that person? Maybe you didn't like how much she talked or the way she spoke to her children. Perhaps she seemed a little stand-off-ish. Or maybe there was just a certain something you couldn't put your finger on. But then after spending more time with that person and really getting to know her, you realized that in spite of a few personality quirks, she was really a great person and you quite liked her after all? This same principle applies to many things in life. The more you know and understand something, the more confident you will feel about, like, and embrace it.

And so it is with our selves. The more you know and understand yourself and the stronger you are connected to Self, the more you will respect and value YOU. This is what true self-esteem is: knowing that you are precious because of *who you are*, not *what you do*. Valuing yourself and feeling good about yourself has very little to do with your titles, appearance, accomplishments, or possessions.

> **As a woman descends to her own depths . . . she finds a strength, a certainty that changes her.**
>
> —JUDITH DUERK, *Circle of Stones*

This is an ego-based notion of self-esteem that says you have to have a certain level of "somebody-ness" before you can really matter and be accepted. This is why so many people frantically search outside of themselves and struggle to create a self they assume they don't have. The reality is that none of us has to create a self. Your somebody-ness is already there. The essential YOU has always been there just waiting to be accepted and appreciated.

EGO: Up Close and Personal

CHARACTERISTICS OF AN OVERZEALOUS EGO

Without the balance of the essential Self, the ego can become quite overzealous, tyrannical even. When this happens the ego becomes a controlling influence in our lives and prevents us from experiencing a deep sense of love, joy, and connection. Here are the main characteristics of a tyrannical ego:

> lives in fear, doubt, and worry
> judges other people
> lacks faith and trust; needs proof
> beats up on "self"
> constantly strives but is never satisfied
> needs to be right
> is desperate for love and acceptance,
> but looks in all the wrong places

As Michael Gurian says in his book, *The Wonder of Girls,* "There is no room for this kind of ego when our children's souls are constantly beckoning for love and attention." Your days are numbered tyrannical ego. You're about to meet your match!

Okay, we've been talking about the difference between you and YOU, self and Self, ego and essence. Now let's get to the heart of this chapter—getting to know YOU. The following exercises are an opportunity for you to reflect on and express all the things that are essentially YOU. I recommend completing them, as well as all the activities and exercises in this chapter, in "The Essence Journal" that is described in this next section. As you complete each exercise, don't overanalyze your responses; there are no right or wrong answers. Let this activity be simple and fun, allowing your answers to flow freely without judgment. Pay attention to the answers that resonate with you and make you *feel* something. If a word or statement doesn't feel quite right, you can always change it later if you find a more fitting way of expressing your Self.

✂ **I am. . .** "I am" are two of the most powerful words we can use for creating a strong connection with Self. Write down all of the qualities that you love about yourself or that you know are true of you. Here are some ideas to get you started:

I exist as I am and that is enough.
—WALT WHITMAN

loving	compassionate	funny	kind
generous	intelligent	supportive	gentle
strong	patient	adventurous	open
ambitious	practical	optimistic	creative
flexible	loyal	resilient	calm
dynamic	persistent	resourceful	caring
courageous	beautiful	insightful	sensitive

❅ **The real me comes through when...** Think back to events and activities that created a special feeling for you at the time they happened—moments where you felt "in sync" and experiences that made you think, "This is the real me. I need to be doing more of this." What were you doing? Who were you with? Where were you? Write down all of the experiences that come to mind. What was it about these moments that resonated with you?

❅ **People love me for...** I know this sounds a little awkward, but it really is quite valuable to reflect on what our closest friends and family members love about us. After all, they are an important source of unconditional love and often times they see the special things in us that we don't see ourselves. Unsure about what they'd say? Try looking at the homemade cards and pictures your children have made for you over the years. Their words and images are wonderful expressions of what they love about you. Or simply ask your friends and family. When they tell you what they love about you, embrace their words and take it all in. Avoid the temptation to dismiss their answers out of modesty or disbelief. They are offering you an important gift for your journey.

> **Who you are is greater than you can imagine.**
>
> —PHYLICIA RASHAD

While this is an exercise in self-discovery, you might consider reciprocating this gift by letting the people in your life know what you love about them. Seldom do we take the time to do this in our lives. We tend to save these kinds of sentiments for weddings and funerals. Don't wait for a rare occasion to share what you really feel about someone. Let loved ones know how special they are and what you love about them while you can, especially your children who are so precious and continuously developing their sense of self. You never know how far the impact of your gift will go.

❅ **I respect and admire...** Make a list of several people you admire and respect. Reflect on each of these people and write down the characteristics and qualities you most admire about them. Most of the time, the qualities and attributes we are drawn to in other people reflect what we love about and want to bring out in ourselves.

Reinvention Practice

THE ESSENCE JOURNAL

If you only ever do one reinvention practice, please, please let it be this one! This fun, creative, and Self-revelationary practice will change your life. I promise.

The purpose of this journal is to create a book that reflects the essence of YOU on every page. To get started you'll need a blank journal or notebook. I recommend a spiral-bound book with tabbed sections and pockets; however, feel free to choose whatever will work for you. Next you'll need to keep your eyes, ears, and heart open as you gather the things that speak to YOU . . .

- quotes, song lyrics, poems, prayers, or book excerpts you love
- magazine pictures, photographs, postcards, or travel brochures that capture your attention and have meaning for you
- personal reflections and insights on lessons learned, the births of your children, significant achievements you've made
- greeting cards, artwork from your children, or notes from your spouse—little things that warm your heart and bring you joy
- ideas or images of what you hope and dream about for the future

Keep in mind that this is a practice to be engaged in over time—it is not a weekend project! Take your time and revel in the process of uncovering what really moves you, what you really think, and what you really feel. In time, you will notice a pattern emerging across the pages. That pattern tells the story of who YOU are as a unique individual. It's the Book of You.

Your Heart's Desire

Let me ask you the question that started my journey of Self-discovery: *What is your heart's desire?* Have you ever thought about that before? Do you even really have a sense of what "your heart's desire" means? I know it took me a while to figure that out. What I discovered is that once you learn to hear the whispers of your heart and your inner Self, the answer becomes quite simple. Your heart's desire is simply what you love, long for, and feel strongly and passionately about.

I know. You're probably thinking, "Easy for you to say. I'd give anything to find my passion." I can't tell you how many Moms have approached me over the years in sheer desperation trying to figure out what they're passionate about. We tend to think about our heart's desire and our passion like some grand elusive concept that once discovered will cause the heavens to open up and magically transform our lives. But passions are not that mystical or magical. They're simply the things that "capture our heart" and bring us meaning, joy, and excitement—time with family, helping someone in need, celebrations, ideas, books, sports, the movie you watch again and again. They are the little things that are all around us everyday. (How our passions get expressed in the world is a different story and dependent on you—your unique personality, the choices you make, and your life circumstances. But more about that later.)

Your passion is what stirs your soul and makes you feel like you're in total harmony with why you showed up here in the first place.

—Dr. Wayne W. Dyer

Barbara De Angelis writes in her book titled *Passion* that "passion is your essential self . . . the source of who you are." Can you see how knowing your heart's desire is essential to being the Mom and woman you're meant to be? And the good news is, you don't have to go very far or spend a ton of money to find it. You don't even have to think! In fact, you cannot *think* your way to your heart's desire. You only need to be willing to listen and ready to feel. Here are some exercises to help you get reacquainted:

- **I love to. . .** Write down the activities and things you love and that bring you joy. Consider the things that come naturally to you as well—things you seem to have a "knack" for. Most often we love the things we have a natural talent for. Here are some suggestions to get you started . . .

design	teach	learn	counsel
write	garden	analyze	explore
travel	problem-solve	build	heal
fix	read	write	paint
entertain	lead	exercise	comfort
inspire	invent	advocate	motivate
organize	persuade	cook	perform

- **I am drawn to. . .** Make a list of the things you find yourself drawn to: sights, sounds, scents, places, people, décor. What are your favorite books and movies? What types of stores do you love to browse in? What kind of people do you

Feel yourself being quietly drawn by the deeper pull of what you truly love.

—Rumi

love spending time with? Who are the people you most want to serve? All of these things provide clues to your heart's desire.

- **When I was a child, I loved to...** Children teach us a lot about being authentic and connecting to our heart's content. Because the ego is still in the early stages of development, children are closely connected to their essential Selves. They know what they love and they just do it, sometimes for hours on end, without any fear or worry about what other people think. They experience a lot of joy and passion as a result.

  Think back to when you were a child. What did you love to do? What was it that you could do for hours on end and nothing else in the world mattered? What did you want to be when you grew up? What was it about these things that captivated you?

As you write down your responses to these exercises, pay attention to themes or commonalities that appear. What do you notice? What are you uncovering about your Self and your heart's desire?

Heart Speak

FINDING INSPIRATION

Inspiration is one of the ways our heart speaks to us. Unlike motivation, which comes from the head and drives us toward external attainment, inspiration comes from the heart and connects us to something deeper and larger than ourselves.

What inspires you? Which iconic figures or everyday people stir something inside of you that makes you say: "I love that!"?

Ever since I was a little girl, I have been inspired by Princess Diana. I loved her quiet strength, her love and compassion for children and people in need, and her determination to do what was right for her own children in spite of the expectations and practices of those around her. I keep a beautiful photograph of Diana with her sons William and Harry when they were young boys on my desk. This picture inspires me and reminds me of everything that is important to me about being a Mom and a woman.

Who or what inspires you to be the Mom and woman you're meant to be? How can you bring the inspiration of these things into your everyday life?

Your Personal Genius

Each of us comes into this world with unique and special gifts to offer. I call the bundle of these gifts your genius. That may sound strange to you—to think that you have a genius. We tend to think of ourselves only in terms of what needs fixing or improving and that genius is something related to IQ scores and Albert Einstein. But in his book, *Setting your Genius Free*, Dick Richards points out that the term genius has a much broader meaning. According to Richards, the Ancient Greeks believed genius was a spirit that was born at the same time as a person. The genius would be carried by that person throughout his or her lifetime and would serve as a source of both direction and protection—a kind of guiding star and guardian angel all wrapped up in one. Who can't get on board with that notion of genius?!

You have a genius—a bundle of special gifts that will guide you as a Mom and woman on your journey. These gifts are your natural talents and abilities, the things that come easily to you without a lot of thought or effort. In fact, your genius may be so easy and natural for you that you don't even realize that it's anything special. It just seems like something you do.

The truth is that those abilities are more than just something you do, they are part of who you are. That's why recognizing and celebrating your gifts and talents is so important to embracing your essential Self.

You've already uncovered some of your natural talents and "knacks" in the previous section when you created your list of things you love to do. Here are some other questions to help you get in touch with your genius . . .

- ❀ **What am I known for?** What do people come to you for help with or advice on? What do people compliment you on and say you're good at?
- ❀ **What is common sense to me that does not seem to be common sense to others?** What are you doing when you catch yourself saying, "Oh, anyone can do that"? Do you get frustrated when other people fail to do something that you think should be common sense?
- ❀ **Where do I shine as a Mom and parent?** What comes naturally and easily to you as a Mom: teaching, motivating, empathizing, comforting, negotiating, story-telling, nurturing, counseling, organizing, decision-making, communicating?

Make note of your talents and gifts as you reflect on each of these questions. Now, looking back on the talents and passions you wrote down from the "Your Heart's Desire" exercise ("*I love to* . . .") along with the list you've just created, ask yourself: "Which of these talents seem to be right at the core of my being? Which ones are essential in a way that I couldn't imagine ME without those gifts?" Narrow your list down to four or five essential talents. This group of gifts and abilities comprises your personal genius.

Having a clear understanding of our talents and gifts will go a long way in our role as Mom. Not only does this knowledge add to our wisdom and confidence as women and mothers, but it also enables us to help our children recognize and appreciate their own gifts and sense of Self. This kind of Self-confidence will serve them extremely well as they go out into the world to become the individuals they were meant to be.

Remember that tapping into our genius, and helping our children do the same, has nothing to do with IQ, making millions of dollars, or winning a Nobel Prize. This is the overzealous ego's notion of genius—how can I use this to achieve "somebody-ness"? I sadly see parents all the time pushing their kids to excel in something—signing them up for multiple activities, spending gobs of money, and going to great lengths to ensure that they are competitive and can be their best. Striving and pushing does not nurture our children's or our own genius. A guiding star/guardian angel cannot be forced. Striving and pushing is merely addressing our ego's need for outer success and accomplishment and its fear of not being enough. Genius unfolds naturally and it will express itself in many ways, shapes, and forms—some big, some small, some obvious, some subtle. Our job is to support and celebrate those gifts and talents and simply allow them to direct us on our journey. This will always be enough.

> **Raise your child to know who he is and guide him in becoming ever more himself. *In the way he should go.* Not in the way you would like him to go in order to validate you.**
> —Stasi Eldridge

The Mommy Diaries

MY STORY: DIFFERENT KIDS, DIFFERENT GIFTS

A large part of my son's gifts lies in his physical genius. This kid was riding a two-wheel bike at the age of three, was tying his shoes at the age of four, and wields a hockey stick and puck in an exceptional way. His genius and passion for physical activity is obvious and well-recognized. It's his "thing."

My daughter's gifts, on the other hand, are much more subtle. Subtle, yet equally brilliant. Her gifts and passions lie in the arts, relationships, and meaningful connections. She feels deeply about people and things, is sensitive to the feelings of others, and becomes very attached to what holds meaning for her. But because these gifts are less obvious and recognized, she had started to feel down because she didn't have an obvious "thing" like her brother.

We've spent a lot of time in our family discussing the different talents and gifts people are born with and appreciating what makes each of us unique—however that genius shows up in the world. I see both of them now developing an insight and confidence in them Selves to the point that they can even laugh about the things that are clearly not their "thing"!

Kelly Pryde, Mom of two and parent coach

___

Putting It All Together

While there is, and always will be, much about our essential Selves that is difficult to define and express, it is helpful to try to pull together everything you've discovered so far on your journey to the centre of the Self. The idea here is to create a general impression of the essential YOU that will serve as a personal compass as you travel along the journey of life and motherhood. For this reason, it's important that your impression resonates with you in some way. Maybe it brings tears to your eyes, makes you laugh, or gives you a sense of peace. When you feel an emotional connection to your essence impression, you'll know you're on the right track.

___

Reinvention Practice

YOUR SELF IMPRESSION

Look back at your responses to the exercises in this chapter (The Essential YOU, Your Heart's Desire, and Your Personal Genius) and for each statement below choose one to three words that best describe YOU. As earlier, ask yourself, "Which qualities/traits seem to be right at the core of my being? Which ones are so essential that I couldn't imagine ME without them?"

- **My unique qualities are** _____
- **When I was a child I loved to** _____
- **What I absolutely love now is** _____
- **I keep being drawn to** _____
- **My genius (what I do effortlessly and shine at) is** _____
  _____
- **The one word that best describes ME is** _____

Using these qualities/traits as a basis, create a personalized collage that depicts the essence of who you are as a unique individual, and you've got your impression. Here's my Self Impression . . .

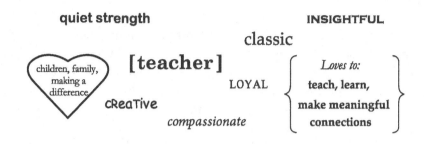

Of course, you'll be adding to and tweaking this impression as you uncover more about your unique Self along your journey. My Self Impression is the culmination of many years of reinvention, self-discovery, and growth. That being said, use this impression as your personal guide and simply modify and add to it when necessary. The important thing is to allow your essential Self to be at the heart of your decision making, your parenting, and your life. When your decisions and actions are grounded in the truth of who you are and what you love about YOU, a deeper level of joy and connection in life is inevitable.

COMING HOME

We've gone deep into the centre of the Self to discover the YOU that's not Mom. What do you think? More importantly, how do you feel? Chances are while you are delighted to have uncovered such rich information about yourself, you may also be feeling slightly unsettled. Maybe even a bit lost, wondering "What do I do with this new knowledge of my Self?" "How do I translate it into my everyday life?" These feelings are perfectly normal. In fact, if you weren't experiencing some uneasiness or ambiguity, I might worry that you haven't fully connected with feeling yet.

> **Once you figure out who you are and what you love about yourself, I think it all kinda falls into place.**
>
> —JENNIFER ANISTON

Empathic writer, Erika Harris, once wrote that "It is good to feel lost . . . because it proves you have a navigational sense of where "Home" is. You know that a place that feels like *being found* exists. And maybe your current location isn't that place but, Hallelujah, that unsettled, uneasy feeling of lost-ness just brought you closer to it." These words are very applicable to this point in your journey. In reconnecting with your inner Self, you now know where "Home" is for you. That place where you *know* you belong and everything just fits. The uneasy, unsettled feelings you're experiencing at this point reflect that your current life situation isn't quite in that place yet, but you know where it is and are anxious to get there. Rest assured, this leg of the reinvention journey has brought you closer to Home.

In many ways this part of the journey is simply a transition like moving into a new house. You know it's the perfect place for you, but it doesn't feel like home yet. Give it time. Explore your new space and experiment with different ways of using it. When something feels right, you'll know. Add your personal touches—your YOU—where you can to reflect what's important to you. This is how you create contentedness and meaning around you. In time, things will come together. You will settle in and the feel of your new space will become more familiar. The important thing is not to obsess about the process and panic about not getting to that place quicker. Be patient and allow things to unfold naturally. If you stay connected to that inner compass, it will always point you towards Home.

> **The project of being a self is the surest way never to feel like a person.**
> —THOMAS MOORE

As you continue towards Home embracing your essential Self, you might feel a tendency to reject your ego self—that part of you that fears, worries, judges, and strives and may now feel like a hindrance. But you don't have to conquer or defeat your ego. It is part of what makes us human and it's important to embrace that part of ourselves, too. Remember that up until now, your ego self has simply been over-developed and run amok from lack of connection and balance with Self. Connection with Self gives us the perspective we need to find meaning and connection in everyday life and to ensure we don't get caught up in the ego's overzealous need to achieve. But the essential Self alone does not make a human life. A healthy and honest connection to the ego self is essential for keeping us grounded in reality and enabling us to fully contribute as Moms and women.

Here is an example of how a disconnection between ego and Self might reveal itself:

A fellow Mom I know believes that she is meant to stay at home to look after her family. And she is brilliant at it. She gets up early every morning to see her husband off to work and her children off to school. She spends her days tending their home and preparing meals for her family, rarely venturing out to engage with friends or community. She is a devoted wife and mother and believes herself to be free of ego in making the choice to stay home. But she is very critical of fellow Moms who choose to work outside the home, believing that they are selfish and have chosen material possessions over family. In fact, she once commented that if all mothers were as loving and committed as she, the world would be a much better place.

The discrepancy in this line of thinking—that we are free of ego *and* somehow better than others—is a perfect example of what visionary writer Oriah has said about needing both our essential and ego selves to live a fully human life: "Essence awareness accepts and holds it all. Ego awareness can sometimes be helpful in identifying the bullshit."

Continue to uncover and connect with your new found Self and allow it to guide your choices about what you do and how you live and parent. But don't ignore or reject your ego self in the process. Be aware of its vulnerabilities and tendencies towards fear, judgment, thoughts of lack, and control, as well as its unique wisdom for keeping you grounded and identifying the bullshit. With an inner compass guiding you Home and a bullshit tracker for keeping it real, how can you go wrong?!

*   *   *   *   *

Reinvention Practice

SEEING YOUR SELF

Find a few minutes of uninterrupted quiet space and sit in a comfortable position. Take a few deep breaths—in and out—and allow your mind to slowly empty of its chatter and activity. When you are ready, allow an image of yourself to come to mind and see yourself at one of your worst moments. Maybe you are losing your temper with one of your children or rejecting your husband because of something he did or didn't do. Maybe you are drinking or eating excessively as a way to repress difficult feelings. Simply watch how the patterns of your ego personality—your "self"—play out for you.

As you see yourself in this moment, allow the behaviors to fall away. See the anger, fear, or sadness disappear and begin to imagine all of the qualities and characteristics you included in your Self Impression—what you love deeply, how you are brilliant, and who YOU are when all else falls away. Stay with this image, smile at what you see, and know that this is who you really are.

When you are able to see yourself as you are and love what you see, then you have discovered true self-acceptance. Welcome home.

REFLECTION AND ACTION FOR PATH FOUR

✖ Consider the ways your Self is currently reflected in your everyday life. Where do you see elements of your essential Self in your roles as Mom, wife, friend, career woman, volunteer, etc.? In what ways are YOU missing from key areas of your life?

✖ Get to know your ego self and resist the habit of letting it run amok in your life. A wise Indian saying advises: "Forget old habits of feeling and thinking; keep telling yourself 'No, not so . . . I am not like this, I do not need it, I don't want it.'" As you become more aware of your ego self, the less influence it will have on you and the more you can tune in to the voice of your essential Self.

✖ In his book, *A New Earth*, Eckhart Tolle writes, "The longing for love that is in every child is the longing to be recognized . . . on the level of Being." In what ways do you recognize your children for who they are rather than for what they do? How can you help your children connect with their essential Selves as they continue to grow and develop?

FURTHER READING FOR PATH FOUR

The Invitation by Oriah Mountain Dreamer (New York: HarperCollins, 1999)

Based on the wisdom of her beloved poem, this book is an invitation to confront the challenges that open us up to love and life, to awaken to our heart's longings, and to live more deeply, honestly and passionately.

Your Sacred Self by Wayne W. Dyer, Ph.D. (New York: HarperCollins, 2001)

Bestselling author and spiritual teacher, Dr. Wayne Dyer offers wisdom and strategies for freeing ourselves from the tyranny of the ego and getting back in touch with our essential sacred selves.

Eat, Pray, Love by Elizabeth Gilbert. (New York: Penguin Group, 2006)

In her beautifully written memoir, Elizabeth Gilbert shares how she made the difficult decision in her thirties to leave behind a successful Manhattan life and embark on a year-long quest across three countries to discover happiness, meaning, and self-love. A definite must-read!

PATH 5

ROMANCING THE SOUL

Re-enchanting Your Everyday Life

You look at that river gently flowing by. You notice the leaves rustling with the wind. You hear the birds; you hear the tree frogs . . . . You feel the grass . . . . It's quiet; it's peaceful. And all of a sudden, it's a gear shift inside you. And it's like taking a deep breath and going, "Oh yeah, I forgot about this."

—AL GORE, *An Inconvenient Truth*

Several years ago when my daughter was about to start Grade One, we decided to go out one Saturday for a girls' day of back-to-school shopping and lunch together. We had a busy, fun-filled day picking out clothes and other essentials for school. By 3:30 in the afternoon, we were both tired and decided to stop for a snack at our local Starbucks. Little did I know this pit stop would be the best part of our entire day.

Rather than sit across from me at our table in Starbucks, my daughter curled up in the seat beside me and nestled her head on my shoulder. For about fifteen minutes, we just sat there. We exchanged few words and just sat together watching some employees rearrange store shelves. It was the most connected we had been all day and we were doing nothing—we were simply being there together. It was a good moment that I've never forgotten.

Those few minutes were like a gear shift for me, reminding me how important it is to slow down and be in the present moment to connect with the simple yet magical things in life—the little moments where our hearts and imaginations are captivated by someone or something. Too often in our hurried lives as Moms, we're so busy running around, getting things done, and checking off our to-do lists that we miss the many opportunities to connect with these special moments—moments that offer us a more contented and joyful way of being. One of my favorite spiritual writers, Thomas Moore, calls these little moments "enchantment." Enchantment. Doesn't that sound wonderful? With all the functional and practical doing we contend with on a daily basis—laundry, errands, diapers, carpooling, career, and tidying—we are all in desperate need of enchantment.

Just like our bodies need food and our minds require thought in order to thrive, our souls need regular excursions into enchantment. Without them, we experience a certain emptiness—that need for something more—as our hearts and souls long for a way of living that is vastly deeper and richer than our everyday hurried existence. Making this deep connection is what the spiritual journey is all about and what we will explore on this pathway. As a rich source of connection, enchantment offers us an essential way of replenishing the spiritual vacancies in our running on empty lifestyle.

> **Enchantment invites us to pause and be arrested by whatever is before us; instead of our doing something, it is done to us.**
> —THOMAS MOORE

THE SPIRITUAL 411: A PRELUDE TO ENCHANTMENT

This might sound strange, but I had a difficult time deciding how to write about this pathway. For many people, the terms *spiritual* and *soul*—and even *enchantment*—are synonymous with religion or new age mysticism which can trigger all kinds of negative or uncomfortable feelings. Since spirituality will be the underlying concept of this chapter, and subsequent chapters, it seemed only logical to explain exactly how I'm using this term, just so we're on the same page.

I have come to believe that while spirituality will always remain a mystery in many ways, it doesn't have to be complex or uncomfortable. It doesn't *have to* be about organized religion, deep meditation, or dancing under a full moon. Spirituality is simply about a connection—an intentional, loving connection to life within and around us. Beloved author and spiritual director Henri Nouwen taught that *spirituality is anything that leads us to slow down and re-focus our time, thoughts, and desires in ways that counteract selfishness, impulsiveness, or hurried fogginess of mind.* For me, this is a perfect way to think about spirituality and I will be using it as our guiding principle for exploring enchantment. In thinking about it this way, spirituality can be experienced in an endless number of ways—laughing, praying, helping someone in need, walking in nature, sharing Thanksgiving dinner . . . or even sitting quietly in Starbucks with your child.

Because we suffer such a great deal from hurried fogginess of mind as Moms, the key to spirituality and enchantment is in awareness—to shift our attention, thoughts, and energy into the present moment and connect with what's happening NOW. That is the only place in which spirituality and enchantment reside. When we can develop our awareness and connect to the present moment, finding enchantment in the beauty and simplicity of things just as they are, many things fall into place and we discover a more loving, joyful, and fulfilled way of being. Isn't this a way of living and being that we truly want for ourselves and our children?

WHY RE-ENCHANTMENT?

When my son was about four years old, he was really into pirates. He dressed up like a pirate, read books about pirates, and played pirate ship adventures. All the time.

The world we want for ourselves and our children will not emerge from electronic speed but rather from a spiritual stillness that takes root in our souls.

—MARIANNE WILLIAMSON

On the days when he wasn't attending Junior Kindergarten, I typically got roped in to dressing up like a pirate and playing pirate ship adventures. On one particular day of playing pirate ship, for what felt like the umpteenth time, my mind was off thinking about all the things I would have rather been doing—email, grocery shopping, writing, and even laundry. (I know, desperate, right?) But it suddenly occurred to me how fortunate I was to be able to spend this time with my son and that it was such a small window of time I would get with him. In no time, he would be grown up and I would be incredibly un-cool to hang out with. With that realization—that awareness—I got my head back into the pirate ship adventure. I ran up and down our staircase wielding my plastic sword and chasing Davy Jones. I used my toughest "aargh" and my best "ahoy" and just had fun as I left all practicality aside for that short time.

Our children can teach us a lot about enchantment. We only have to watch them laughing, playing, and marveling at the world around them to remember what enchantment and being in the moment look like. Enchantment and present-moment awareness were once second nature to us, too. But as we grew up, we were educated out of it as we learned to set goals and focus onward and upward. And then as Moms, we are whisked out of it daily as the whirlwind constantly pulls us outward in all directions. This is the main reason I used the term re-enchantment for this pathway—it requires us to look to our children who are experts in enchantment, unlearn many of the disenchanted values and ways of thinking we've acquired over the years, and remember how to connect with the ordinary and simple pleasures that are readily available to us everyday.

Along this path, we will explore many sources of enchantment that you can try in your own life—the joyful simplicities of beauty, nature, and art; the comfort of home, family, and ritual; the art of doing nothing; and the power of gratitude. Remember that consistent with all the pathways of reinvention, there isn't a one size fits all approach here. Just as physical fitness requires us to nourish our bodies with food and movement that works for us as unique individuals, so too does spiritual fitness require us to nourish our souls by connecting to life in ways that feel right to each of us as individual Moms and women. Choose the approaches that feel right for you and make the connection.

Seat of the Soul

THE ART AND SCIENCE OF THE HEART

We know that the heart loves and feels, but over the last couple of decades fascinating research has shown that the heart also thinks, remembers, communicates with other hearts and minds, and transmits electromagnetic or "energy" information to the brain and throughout the body.

Running around 24/7 stressed, frazzled, and out of sync? The heart, too, will be out of sync. It will not only generate an uneven rhythmic pattern, but also impede the flow of physiological information to your body and mind, as well as hinder the flow of energy information to the hearts and minds of those around you.

If you change gears to a state of love, gratitude, or pleasure, however, the heart will process those energies and shift to a state of coherence and harmony. It will send that harmonious information throughout your entire body providing many benefits such as increased vitality, mental clarity, and intuition. It will also enhance the flow of energy to the hearts and minds of those around you.

The next time you're feeling frazzled and out-of-sorts, try re-enchanting your heart. Take a minute or two to shift to a feeling of genuine love or appreciation for someone or something in your life and hold that thought. You'll be reconnecting to life in a big way.

Sources: Institute of HeartMath (2001). Science of the Heart. Boulder Creek, CA; Pearsall, P. (1999). The Heart's Code. New York: Broadway Books.

FINDING ENCHANTMENT IN EVERYDAY LIFE

As a spiritual experience, enchantment can be found everywhere and anytime. You only need to pay attention and connect with what's right in front of you in an open-minded, open-hearted way. Here is just a handful of the many ways in which you can nourish your soul and re-enchant your everyday life . . .

Joyful Simplicities

When I began my own reinvention journey more than ten years ago, finding joyful simplicities was one of the primary ways I began to re-connect with feeling and soul. I owe this discovery to a wonderful book by Sarah Ban Breathnach called *Simple Abundance: A Daybook of Comfort and Joy.*

In this bestselling book, Ms. Breathnach offers 366 essays on how to find joyful simplicities—one for every day of the year, plus one for good measure. (Note: If you don't have a copy of this book, I highly recommend it. It makes a wonderful gift for yourself and other special women in your life.) Among her favorites are: making a batch of old-fashioned chocolate fudge, creating a sacred space, roaming antique shops, and reading good books in bed. Oh yes, joyful simplicities are good food for the soul.

As a Mom and woman, I thrive on joyful simplicities—both for myself and with my family. They have become second nature to me. And even though there certainly are days, and sadly sometimes even weeks, where finding a joyful simplicity is the furthest thing from mind, more often than not I relish in several on a daily basis. Here are some of my favorite joyful simplicities that you, too, can find in your everyday life:

- *Nature.* I have a neighbor who complains all summer long about gardening: "Ugghhh. Whoever said gardening is therapeutic is out of their mind!" I always chuckle to myself and think, "You're going about it all wrong." While you don't have to have a green thumb by any means, there is a lot of enchantment to be found in nature . . . if you're open to it. As a prime source of spiritual life, nature invites us into reflection, wonder, and beauty: going for a walk and taking in the rich, vibrant colors of the fall; enjoying the gentle sound of wind chimes or having fresh cut flowers on the kitchen table; star-gazing, having cloud races, or marveling at a magnificent sunset; noticing the smell of fresh cut grass; building a snowman and having hot cocoa with marshmallows afterwards; visiting a farmer's market for fresh picked fruit and filling them in a bowl on your kitchen counter. There is much wisdom in the Persian proverb that says: "If you have but two coins, use one for bread to feed the body and the other for hyacinths to feed the soul." There is simply no shortage of enchantment to be found in nature.

  > When communing with nature, the complexities of life seem to drop away and we remember how simple it really is.
  >
  > —Sylvia Brallier

- *Art.* There is something not only joyfully simple about art, but also magical. Depending on the artist and beholder, art has the power to be anything from aesthetically pleasing to personally meaningful to soulfully enriching. Whether in the form of paintings, photographs, books, music, film, furniture, or design and décor, our lives can be enriched and made spiritually alive through the magic of art.

  When my husband and I bought our first home, we had many walls and spaces that remained bare for months, and even years, until we found just the right pieces to fill those spaces. It was important to me to find art pieces that were not necessarily elaborate or expensive, but would infuse our space with enchantment. All these years later, our home and yard is dappled with many joyful simplicities: arrangements of family photographs, French impressionist artwork, a Celtic cross in our back garden that I can see from our kitchen window, displays of books—everywhere, a crystal fruit basket that belonged to my grandmother, and, of course, artwork that my children have made over the years which have such a wonderful energy about them.

Art washes away from the soul the dust of everyday life.
—PABLO PICASSO

Look around you. What works of art are in your everyday space that offer you little moments of enchantment?

- *Random delights.* Here are some other simplicities that can bring you and your loved ones real moments of connection, comfort, and joy:

  ❖ Watching a funny movie that makes you laugh hysterically.
  ❖ Having two-minute family snuggles before you get out of bed to start the day.
  ❖ Drinking a latté with lots of foam and cinnamon sprinkles over a chat with a close friend.
  ❖ Lighting scented candles around your home. Orange-cranberry, ginger peach, vanilla sugar, baked apple pie. Need I say more?
  ❖ Curling up with your children to read a bedtime story.
  ❖ Eating a dark chocolate truffle. Slowly.
  ❖ Pulling out your good china and having a special family dinner, just because.
  ❖ A warm, scented bubble bath. How enchanting is it to soak in a tub with a glass of wine and a good book, surrounded by candles and scented bubbles? Simply joyful.

Reinvention Practice

YOUR PERFECT HAPPINESS

Broadcast journalist Katie Couric once commented, "My idea of perfect happiness is sitting at the kitchen table laughing with my daughters." What is your idea of "perfect happiness"?

Too often we wrap our ideas of happiness around accomplishments and the acquisition of things—a career promotion, a new kitchen, or a fancy vacation. And while these things can certainly bring us a brief moment of happiness, this kind of happiness is fleeting and only mildly satisfactory.

"Perfect happiness" is a deeper, more meaningful kind of happiness—it's joy. It involves connection, love, and being and can be found in everyday ordinary moments. Think of at least three of your perfect happiness experiences and consider what about them brings you that deeper feeling of joy. How easy it for you to experience these moments of joy in your everyday life? How often do you notice them as *joy*?

No Place Like Home

Ask anyone who knows me and they will tell you that I am not a domestic person! I get grumpy about cleaning, tend to leave piles of things around the house, put off folding the laundry, and have never particularly enjoyed cooking. Chances are that you relate to some of these sentiments, too. But even though a June Cleaver or Martha Stewart I am not, I do know the importance of and work towards creating a home that is a "soft place to fall."

Creating a home that is a soft place to fall has little to do with money, furniture, or upgrades and everything to do with the energy and emotion you invest in it. It's about creating an energy that is warm, loving, safe, and content. It's about creating a space that is authentic and real, reflecting who you are as a family and what you value together. And it's about creating a sense of belonging so that no matter what happens in the outside world, home is the place where you know you will always be accepted and cherished unconditionally.

Home as an emotional and spiritual experience—a place where family, belonging, security, memory and personal history abide—cannot be bought. You can only create it with the investment of your time, intention, and loving energy.

While there are always things I'd like to change and do around our home, many of these to-do's are in the long-range forecast; they're nice-to-haves that we'll get to in time. There are, however, four must-have practices that I try to ensure are on the daily or at least regular agenda—practices that I feel contribute greatly to a sense of enchantment and a soft place to fall in our home:

1. *Make it beautiful and meaningful.* As I mentioned earlier, beautiful doesn't mean expensive or trendy—it means anything that has meaning and significance for you and your family. I've been in many homes that are beautiful in the sense that they are "picture-perfect," like something out of a magazine, but they say nothing about the family that lives there—who they are or what their

> **Choose things because they delight you, not because they impress others.**
> —MARNEY MORRIS

interests are. These homes are designed to impress rather than enchant. Make your home a beautiful reflection of who you are, not who you think you should be. Creating a home that is warm, cozy, meaningful, and inviting for you and your family with what you have now is one of the most important practices you can do to create a sense of enchantment in your home.

Equally important is to allow your children to create spaces that are unique reflections of who they are and what's important to them. Remember that beauty is in the eye of the beholder. While posters on the wall and rock collections may not speak to your soul, it may speak volumes to theirs. Be flexible and willing to let them experiment with what is meaningful to them in their space. My general rule of thumb when it comes to picking battles with my kids is that if it's not physically, emotionally, or ethically harmful, let it go.

2. *Keep it simple.* There's no denying that most of us have too much clutter in our lives—cluttered closets, cluttered drawers, cluttered calendars, cluttered minds. Unfortunately, out of all this clutter comes chaos, uncertainty, and disenchantment—ingredients that do not make for a soft place to fall. We can all do better at cleaning up the clutter in our lives by purging extraneous items and creating order with the basics we need; by slowing down and simplifying our schedules; and by ridding our thoughts of meaningless details so we can more easily focus on the things that really matter to us. We'll explore the topic of simplicity in greater detail in Path Six on the art of letting go, but for now practicing this kind of simplicity in our homes allows us to create a greater sense of peace and comfort for ourselves and our family.

So where do you have clutter in your home that can be cleared out? A drawer? A closet? An entire room? C'mon, you know you have it. Ignoring it won't make it go away! Trust me. I'm right there in denial-ville with you. But I know that if we tackle just *one* junk drawer or *one* pile of stuff, we'll open the doors for enchantment, and many other blessings, to come into our lives.

3. *Practice rituals and traditions.* If you think back to fond memories you have growing up, many of them will revolve around family rituals—Sunday dinner, birthdays, family vacations, and holidays. Rituals and traditions are a powerful source of enchantment and are essential to us as social, emotional, and spiritual beings. Rituals create security, contentment, meaning, and a sense of belonging—some of our most basic human needs—when they are performed with intention and an open heart.

> **There is magic in the family meal. . . . So pull up some chairs. Lose the TV. Let the phone go unanswered. And see where the moment takes you.**
>
> —NANCY GIBBS

In our homes and our daily lives, it's very easy to engage in rituals and traditions that are both meaningful and fun for our families. Group hugs, bedtime snuggles, pajama days, Sunday brunch, Taco Tuesdays, movie night—these are just a few simple rituals you can do to re-enchant your everyday life. Simply having dinner together as a family on a regular basis is good for the mind, body, and soul. Research has shown us time and again that family mealtime rituals are associated with stronger family relationships, healthier children, as well as increased social skills and academic achievement. And yes, even those "chaotic, spilled milk, you're-not-leaving-til-you-eat-your-vegetables" meals can qualify as enchantment if we embrace them with an open heart.

The Convenience Problem

THE DISENCHANTMENT OF MODERN CONVENIENCE

With all of the conveniences readily available to us today, we have adopted a fast-paced, no frills, assembly-line kind of lifestyle. All too often we are hooked on efficiency and speed with not enough time or inclination for family traditions and the little things that draw families together and bring soul, love, and enchantment to life.

Consider these facts . . .

- For many families, cars have replaced the hearth as the center of family life. This trend was highlighted in a recent magazine article offering 2-minute techniques for connecting with your kids in the car as well as in a statistic showing that 1 out of 5 meals is eaten in the car.
- With both parents working and the constant shuttling of kids to sports and activities, the family dinner is becoming a lost tradition. Even when families do eat together, research shows that most meals last 20 minutes or less and that many families are watching TV during that time.
- With the huge increase in electronic media use—multiple TVs in the house (including the kitchen and bedrooms), texting, on-line social networking, and video games—face-to-face interaction and family time has declined significantly.

These facts only confirm what we already know deep in our hearts: Unhurried time together as a family enriches our lives and the lives of our children. There is sacredness in routinely preparing and eating meals together. There is charm in sitting around a table playing a family board game and tucking our children in at night with a bedtime story. We only have to slow down and connect with those things that truly matter to us.

4. *Redefine housework.* Okay, this practice is one that I *try*—really hard—to engage in at home. As I mentioned, housework makes me grumpy. I'm sure it does for you, too. Recent research shows that housework is one of the foremost tasks that makes us unhappy. No kidding. It's pure drudgery, isn't it?

Or is it?

In *Simple Abundance*, Sarah Ban Breathnach reminds us that the time, energy, and emotion we invest daily in our homes for ourselves and our loved ones can be a sacred endeavor. We choose the energy and emotion we put into our homes and lives. And that means we can prepare the meals, make the beds, and dust the furniture in protest and irritation or with willingness and care. Breathnach suggests that we stop calling our daily round "housework" and begin calling it "homecare." In this way, the seemingly ordinary, insignificant tasks we do everyday become a source of enchantment rather than disenchantment; they add to the heart and soul of our homes and our lives rather than to the hustle, bustle, and drudgery.

> **The ordinary acts we practice everyday at home are of more importance to the soul than their simplicity might suggest.**
> —THOMAS MOORE

Now, I know what you're thinking. "She's gone off the deep end on this one." And I fully understand how you would come to that conclusion. I remember seeing an episode of Oprah years ago where a woman described how doing her laundry was a spiritual event for her. She actually had a Buddha statue sitting on her dryer and folded clothes by candlelight. I couldn't help but think, "What-ever." What I didn't realize at the time was that I hadn't yet discovered enchantment. It wasn't until many years later that I finally got it: When you open yourself up to enchantment, sometimes it just finds you, even in the most unexpected places.

The Mommy Diaries

A PLACE FOR EVERYTHING

I have always enjoyed housework and never thought of it as drudgery. My homes have always been a part of me, so the state of my home affects my mood and outlook on a daily basis.

Just like scented candles and quiet music calm us, a clean and tidy house calms me. When the house is constantly messy with things out of order, then my mood is darker and my thoughts are helter-skelter. When everything is tidy and in its place, then so are my thoughts. I feel peaceful and I find my days more productive and "on purpose."

That's not to say that I obsess over a clean house. I decided a long time ago that there will be days when I simply choose not to tidy or clean anything. I can look at my house cluttered with kids' toys and books and know that I would not trade that for anything. Where everything in its place can bring calmness and harmony, a mess can bring a sense of family, joy, and comfort.

Leslie Pighin, Mom of four, Grandma of four, and registered nurse

---

For a variety of reasons, we tend to waste a lot of our time and energy on the things we don't like and wish we could change about our homes—a new sofa, a fresh coat of paint, newer flooring, less tidying and cleaning. In doing so, we create a lot of disenchantment for ourselves and our family. Spend more time and energy on the things you do love about your home, not to mention the fact that you even have one during these uncertain times. When you look on your home with love and thanks, you create the kind of haven you and your family truly need.

> **Be grateful for the home you have, knowing that, at this moment, all you have is all you truly need.**
> —Sarah Ban Breathnach

Il Bel Far Niente

At the beginning of this pathway, I shared the story of spending a few quiet moments with my daughter where we did absolutely nothing, yet were incredibly content. Italians have a beautiful expression for this . . . it's called *il bel far niente* which means "the beauty of doing nothing." I love that. There is a lot of beauty and enchantment to be found in doing nothing.

For most Moms who live in a state of perpetual busyness, the thought of doing nothing is a foreign concept. In fact, for many, it creates a feeling of uneasiness and even panic. We feel like we *need* to be doing something because doing nothing is simply unproductive. Our culture works some of the longest, most stressful hours in the world today, all because we've been ingrained with this notion of productivity and constant doing. We really don't know how to find pleasure, contentment, and enchantment in nothing.

Until today.

Il bel far niente doesn't mean we stop working hard. It simply means that we stop working and doing and going *all the time*. It means that we learn how to shift gears from the mad pace of our daily lives to a slower, richer way of being for a short time. You don't have to be rich or take extravagant vacations to experience the beauty of doing nothing either. In fact, most families I know that go on vacation to escape the busyness of their everyday lives return in desperate need of a vacation from their vacation. After hours of packing and traveling and days of living out of suitcases and sightseeing, most people—at least parents anyway—arrive home utterly exhausted.

The beauty of doing nothing is simple. It's about stripping life down to the bare essentials and finding contentment, connection, and serenity there. Here are some ways you can experience il bel far niente—the beauty of doing nothing—for yourself and your family:

❖ *Have a pajama day.* On a cold wintry day or a lazy Sunday, make a big bowl of popcorn and watch movies with your family under a big blanket. This is one of my family's most favorite ways of doing nothing.

❖ *Try piddling.* Celebrated poet Maya Angelou once described the art of piddling as the practice of just sitting or puttering around for no other reason than just because. Enjoying a cup of tea in the early morning before the rest of the world awakes, going for a quiet walk on your lunch break, collecting cool rocks with your toddler—these are all forms of piddling. Our teens also know a thing or two about piddling. Try following their lead for a few moments during the day, willingly and with an open heart, and enchantment is sure to find you.

Nothing isn't an absence . . . it's a presence.

—Barbara Kingsolver, *Prodigal Summer*

❖ *Go on a picnic.* Picnics are a simple way to just be with family and do nothing. Well, almost nothing. Pack a basket or cooler with a few sandwiches, a freshly sliced watermelon and some lemonade (read: minimal preparation), grab a blanket, a book, and a few toys, and head to a local park. There's nothing like an old fashioned family picnic for getting back to basics and enjoying the beauty of nothing. (Note: cell phones and electronic devices are not allowed!)

❖ *Stay in bed.* I know this is much easier said than done when you have little ones at home. But for just one morning, arrange for Dad or a family member to take the kids and stay in bed without guilt or worry about not getting things done. There is much spiritual power in sleep, so even though nothing may be getting done on the outside, know that there's a whole lot getting done on the inside. Just sleep. And allow contentment to inhabit every ounce of your being.

The French poet Guillaume Apollinaire reminds us that "Now and then, it's good to pause in our pursuit of happiness and just be happy." The beauty of doing nothing is a wonderful way to heed this wisdom, to just be still and allow enchantment and contentment to come to us.

Your G-Spot

Okay, now that I've got your attention, let me reassure you (or maybe disappoint you) that I'm not talking about *that* G-spot. I'm actually referring to gratitude here—the mental and spiritual state of being grateful. Unfortunately, the concept of gratitude has become somewhat of a cliché over the last decade or so. We've all heard about the importance of gratitude and how it enhances mood, happiness, and well-being. And sure, we extend thanks and appreciation for kindnesses that are afforded to us. But for many of us, the idea of a regular gratitude practice is simply one more thing to add to our to-do lists. As a result, it tends to fall by the wayside along with the organic vegetable garden, the breadmaker, and the membership to the gym we had such good intentions for.

Seeing gratitude as an obligation and to-do is exactly how we continue to disenchant our lives. For a state of true gratitude, above and beyond rote thank-you's and social etiquette, is a very rich and enchanting experience. It allows us to turn the ordinary into the extraordinary. It allows us to find depth and reverence in a world that often only sees the flat surfaces in life—material things, financial security, accomplishments, and appearances.

Consider this: How many times in a day do you focus on needing more, wanting more, or complaining about something versus having enough and loving things exactly as they are? Chances are you focus on what you lack and dislike significantly more often than not. It just seems to be in our nature. American writer John Updike once commented, "Our brains are no longer conditioned for reverence and awe." Gratitude is what re-trains our brains, and our hearts we now know, to tune in so we can recognize and appreciate the beauty and abundance that surrounds us every day.

But how do we re-train our brains and our hearts for gratitude? This is where the practice comes in. We pick up our journals, look around, and start taking stock of the many blessings in our lives, all the riches and abundance we take for granted on a daily basis: a loving partner; beautiful children; a comfortable home; a warm bed to curl up in; food in the refrigerator; clean water; family and friends who love us; furry friends that bring us joy and companionship; someone to hug and whisper "I love you" to at the end of the day. And the list goes on and on.

> **Gratitude unlocks the fullness of life. It turns what we have into enough, and more.**
> —Melody Beattie

When we can open our eyes and hearts to consciously and routinely notice and appreciate all the abundance in our lives, our brains change. And we change. We become less judgmental and more accepting, less frazzled and calmer, less disconnected and more loving. We are able to find the extraordinary in everyday ordinary things.

This may sound completely absurd, but shortly after I began a gratitude practice many years ago, I actually recall washing dishes one evening after dinner and smiling, thinking how grateful I was for our pots and pans. Yes that's right. My pots. We had received them as a wedding gift and they just washed so darn easily. I was literally grateful for my pots and had found enchantment in doing the dishes. When you can find a little moment of happiness in something as mundane as washing the dishes, you know you're a changed person. Enchantment will find you just about anywhere.

Reinvention Practice

CULTIVATING A GRATEFUL HEART

Shifting our thoughts and feelings from the lack and annoyances to the abundance and riches in our lives takes practice. Here are some ways you can begin to make this inner shift . . .

Write it down: In *Simple Abundance,* Sarah Ban Breathnach is adamant about writing down five things that you are grateful for every day. She states that if you want to travel any transformative journey, daily gratitude is simply not an option. From my personal experience, I wholeheartedly agree. Writing down joyful simplicities and blessings you are thankful for is the first step in shifting your thoughts and feelings from lack to riches. This is also a great practice to do with your children at bedtime.

Grace before meals: Even if you're not particularly religious, saying grace before meals is a wonderful ritual to connect family members in the present moment and offer thanks for the food before you. There are dozens of mealtime prayers, sayings, and poems to choose from. Choose one that is meaningful for your family, express your words of thanks before you eat . . . then pass the rolls.

Try guerilla gratitude: This is not your everyday, typical gratitude. This is out-of-the-norm, I could have easily NOT done that gratitude. Write a thank you note to your husband or kids, your kids' teacher, coach, or bus driver, or the person who styles your hair. Thank people for and comment on the excellent service they offer at the grocery store, in a restaurant, or at the mall. Blow people away with your guerilla gratitude.

Accept gratitude: Many people have as much trouble accepting thanks as they do compliments and help from others. A grateful heart is a revolving door: gratitude goes out *and* comes in. When someone offers you thanks, don't shrug it off with "It was nothing" or "Oh, I really didn't do anything." Open your heart, accept it, and say "You're welcome," which literally means, "You are received."

LIFE IS IN THE MOMENTS

One of my favorite sayings is, "Life is not measured by the number of breaths we take, but by the number of moments that take our breath away." The moments that take our breath away are where we find enchantment, joy, and meaning in our lives. You don't need a lot of money, a big house, or an extravagant lifestyle to experience these moments. They are available to each of us everyday. You only have to connect with them.

There is a beautiful story about a young girl whose mother had been diagnosed with terminal cancer. With only a short time to live, her family decided to drop everything and travel around the world for an entire year so they could be together and make the most of the remaining time they had with their Mom. They traveled to European countries, Africa, Disneyland, and Hawaii taking in some of the world's most beautiful sights and experiences while breathing in and savoring every moment they had together.

Shortly after her mother passed away, the young girl was asked about what she remembered most about that year with her mother. Rather than talk about all the amazing places they visited, the girl recounted a quiet afternoon with her Mom while the rest of the family was down at the beach. Her Mom wasn't feeling particularly well that day and had asked her daughter to bring her a bowl of Cheerios in bed. Those few moments sitting in bed eating Cheerios with her Mom was the most special memory she had of that time with her.

A shared bowl of Cheerios. It really is that simple.

The Mommy Diaries

FOOTPRINTS ON THE HEART

Last summer, my husband and I couldn't afford to take our family on vacation. I was crushed. I was so disappointed and guilt-ridden because I felt like we wouldn't be providing our kids with good childhood memories. Luckily, my best (and very wise) friend reminded me that *our children won't remember what we said or what we did, but they will remember how we made them feel.*

This advice made me realize that the happiness, excitement, and togetherness that come from an elaborate, expensive vacation could be found just about anywhere. Instead of our big vacation, we went camping at a nearby national park. We borrowed camping supplies from friends and family and we spent a week in the great outdoors hiking, swimming, telling stories, and eating s'mores. More than a year later, my kids are still talking about how our family camping trip was the best time they ever had. I'm convinced it left a deep footprint on their hearts.

Janet, Mom of three and sales rep

Life really is about the little moments that capture our hearts. And the truth is, whether it's five or twenty-five years from now, we won't remember the details about what we wore, who said what, or how tidy the house was. Neither will our children. What we will remember are the little moments where we felt contentment, comfort, love, and a sense of belonging. These are the moments that are imprinted in our heart's memory. And the only way to experience these deeper, richer feelings and create lasting memories is to slow down and tune in to what we're doing and why we're doing it. When we get too caught up in the hustle and bustle of everyday life and run on adrenaline to get everything done, we literally cut ourselves off from the opportunity to connect with these moments. That's the very nature of how adrenaline works in our bodies—it serves to disconnect us from how we're feeling and what we remember, a state that couldn't be further from what enchantment is all about.

*　*　*　*　*

Several years ago for my birthday, my daughter, who was seven at the time, made me a special card that has become one of my favorite treasures. It reads:

> *Happy Birthday Mommy!*
> *When I was born, you were the best thing*
> *that I saw because you were very*
> *pretty and beautiful and I want you*
> *to be happy with your life and*
> *your present. I love you and you*
> *have a great birthday.*
> *Sincerely, love, Marei. xoxoxoxo*

Heart captured. Soul touched. Pure enchantment.

REFLECTION AND ACTION FOR PATH FIVE

- Take some time to discover the joyful simplicities that bring you comfort and contentment. A walk in the woods, curling up with a cozy blanket and a good book on a rainy day, wrapping your little ones in a big fluffy towel as they step out of the bath, a glass of wine with your partner after the kids have gone to bed. Whatever your simple pleasures are, tune in and delight in them. You'll be giving your soul—and your family—a wonderful gift.

- Take an inventory of your home and decide where you can invest some more love and "homecare." What does your family love and find meaningful in your home? Do you have sources of disenchantment that can be cleared out? Is there a family ritual you'd like to begin? Perhaps you have one from your own childhood that you can continue. Focusing on any of these areas will add a whole new level of love, warmth, and enchantment to your life.

- How much time does your family have for *il bel far niente*? How might you clear your calendar clutter to make time for doing nothing? Are you and/or your children overscheduled? Where can you say "no" to more doing so you can say "yes" to some nothing?

FURTHER READING FOR PATH FIVE

Gift from the Sea by Anne Morrow Lindbergh (New York: Pantheon Books, 1955)

In this beloved, timeless memoir the author shares her wisdom and insight on simplicity, peaceful solitude, contentment, care of the soul, and the shape of a woman's life throughout marriage and motherhood during a brief vacation by the sea.

Simple Abundance by Sarah Ban Breathnach (New York: Bantam Dell, 2006)

A book of 366 provocative essays—one for every day of the year—written for women who want to live with more peace, contentment, and authenticity.

Serenity Prayers by June Cotnam (New York: Bantam Dell, 2006)

A lovely collection of prayers, prose, and poems that inspires readers to feel more peace and serenity in their lives. Includes the voices of writers such as Rumi, Walt Whitman, Emily Dickinson and Mitch Albom.

The Family Dinner by Laurie David (New York: Hachette Book Group, 2010)

Film and TV producer and Mom of two Laurie David offers a variety of fresh ideas and research from more than 50 child-care experts and celebrities in support of family mealtime rituals.

Care of the Soul: A Guide for Creating Depth and Sacredness in Everyday Life by Thomas Moore (New York: HarperPerennial, 1994)

In this beautifully written, bestselling book by a renowned theologian and former Catholic Monk, Moore offers an approach to living that challenges us to restore our spiritual lives by finding the sacredness in everyday life.

PATH 6

The Art of Letting Go

Rethinking Balance and Priorities

The Universal Mom To-Do List:

1. *Re-schedule kids' dentist appointments*
2. *Pick up groceries*
3. *Do banking*
4. *Call Aunt Bev*
5. *Take Emily to piano*
6. *Get bristol board for Jay's school project*
7. *RSVP for Dillon's birthday*
8. *Work out*
9. *Lose 10 lbs.*
10. *Fight aging*

Balance. Of all the issues I discuss with fellow Moms, struggling with life balance while not having enough time to get everything done is at the top of the list. "How do I find balance in the midst of a career, children, marriage, laundry, shopping, homework, soccer practice, family, friends, and community? It's too much." "I constantly feel like I'm being pulled in all directions" "There's never enough time in the day to get it all done." "What the heck is this thing called *balance*?! Is there even such a thing?"

While we may feel that our struggle to find life balance comes from a lack of time, it certainly does not come from a lack of trying. In our efforts to find balance and get everything done, we've learned a multitude of ways to manage time, create checklists, prioritize our lives, and be more organized and productive. But the more we struggle to balance and manage our lives, the more balance seems to elude us. And the more balance slips through our fingers, the more anxious, guilty, and running on empty we feel about not getting it all done. This is not how we're meant to be living.

The truth is: Life is not meant to be managed and under control at all times. There is no balance! Striving for balance and juggling priorities is like trying to hold a beach ball underwater—it's exhausting and futile. It will always elude us. Sometimes it will even snap back unexpectedly and smack us square in the face. In the end, all this struggling just wears us out and disconnects us from the things that truly matter to us. For this reason, we're going to be turning the traditional notion of balance on its head on this pathway. You will have the opportunity to not only rethink balance and priorities, but also relinquish your need to be in control and always "keep up," as well as to let go of things that no longer hold any meaning for you.

There is no balance. Let's find out how to make the best of this lopsided world of motherhood by discovering a calmer, more effortless approach to life.

> **There is no balance. You have to make the best of it because it's always lopsided.**
>
> —JENNY McCARTHY on motherhood

LESSONS IN BALANCE

I started rethinking the whole idea of balance several years ago on a trip to Cuba where I learned some valuable lessons related to balance and priorities. It was the first trip my husband and I had taken together since our children had been born and we were going for a full seven days. To be honest, (and yes, I am embarrassed to admit this), I really wasn't that keen on going. As much as I wanted to go on a trip with my husband, I had just started my business and I had a long list of to-do's I wanted to take care of, not to mention all the planning and organization that was required to leave our kids for a whole week. But as much as it felt like an inconvenience, my husband had won the trip, so it seemed foolish to pass it up. I halfheartedly agreed to go.

In hindsight, that was Lesson #1: *Anytime you want to pass up a vacation, especially a free one, over work and to-do's, life balance ain't working!* At the time though, my sentiments to want to invest more time in a business I loved and had worked very hard to create seemed logical. So I packed my laptop along with my list of to-do's. Little did I know, the laptop and the list would not see the light of day during our trip.

Once in Cuba, I figured I would spend a couple of days lounging on the beach and experiencing the local culture. The resort was all-inclusive, so I definitely planned for time to enjoy a few of those drinks with the little umbrellas. Okay, so maybe I'd spend a few days lounging. Knowing myself and my work ethic, however, I knew I would soon be bored with doing nothing and itching to crack open my laptop and get some work done. But after all this planning and forethought about how I would spend my time, a dastardly thing happened . . .

. . . Cuba changed my mind.

I don't mean it simply changed my mind about working on vacation. Well it did, but it was so much more than that. There was something about sitting beside the ocean listening to the waves crash along the shore, watching a magnificent sunset on an endless horizon, and experiencing the simplicity and richness of the Cuban culture that taught me that I didn't know the first thing about living in balance. Lesson #2 revealed itself in my realization that: *Living in balance has very little to do with checklists and to-do's. And it has absolutely nothing do with control. It does have everything to do with connecting to a more natural way of life—a way that is simple and effortless, a kind of flow that we can connect with at any given moment.* It seemed to me that being connected to this flow was far superior to any notion of balance I knew of. I started wondering how I could experience this flow in my own life.

Okay, at this point you're probably thinking I came up with all of this after one too many of those drinks with the little umbrellas. So let me explain myself to convince you that I was (and am as I write this) completely sober . . .

One of the things to know about Cuba, if you've never been there, is that the culture is completely unlike our own (that is, as a highly industrialized country). Firstly, because of its history, Cuba has retained, and continues to preserve, the natural beauty of the land. Turquoise water, white sandy beaches, and lush green landscapes can be seen just about everywhere you go.

Look! Look deep into nature and you will understand everything.

—ALBERT EINSTEIN

Secondly, there is a pureness and simplicity about the way of life in Cuba that is so appealing and refreshing. There isn't any advertising or commercialism. There is very limited media available. Time is an afterthought. And there is a laidback playfulness about the Cuban people.

Now contrast this to my experience upon arrival back in Canada: concrete, billboards, hurriedness, concrete, noise. More concrete. More advertising. More busyness. Did I mention all the concrete? There's such an unnatural complexity and over-stimulation in our industrialized culture that I had apparently become numb to. After only a week away, I found my brain struggling to sort out and juggle all of the complexities and stimuli that bombarded me. Lesson #3 began to unfold as I realized that we are so busy and over-stimulated in our fast-paced culture that balance as we know it in the form of planners, checklists, schedules, and carpools has become a necessity just for keeping up with the whirlwind. It is a process we use to make juggling *seem* as efficient as possible and to keep life on an even keel. You know, so it doesn't fly off the rails.

As I pondered the stark contrast between the Cuban culture and our way of living on the ride home from the airport, I was reminded of the opening quote of Allison Pearson's novel *I Don't Know How She Does It* which had struck a chord with me a couple of years earlier. (Note: If you've never read this book, it is a hilarious look at the struggles of a working mother as she tries to find the right balance between career and home and the self-doubt she feels about not being able to succeed at both. A great read.) The opening quote of the book reads:

> **juggle:** v. & n. **v. 1** intr. Perform feats of dexterity, esp. by tossing objects in the air and catching them . . . **2** tr. Continue to deal with (several activities at once), esp. with ingenuity. **3** intr. & tr. (foll. by with) **a** to deceive or cheat. **b** misrepresent (facts) . . . **n. 1** a piece of juggling. **2** a fraud.

—Concise Oxford Dictionary

When I first read this definition, I distinctly remember thinking: *To deceive or cheat? Misrepresent? A fraud?* As a working mother, I could certainly relate to the term "juggle" in my own struggle for life balance, but I had never associated this process with deceit or fraud. But the more I thought about it and connected it to my revelations in Cuba, the more I was convinced that there was something very inauthentic about this thing called balance and how we go about trying to achieve it.

In my own efforts to maintain balance and get everything done, I spent so much time trying to keep up and do the übermom thing, that I had slowly become disconnected from why I was doing any of it. How many times had I scrambled to get something done only with the intent of being able to scratch it off my to-do list? How many times had I spent leisure time with my family only to have my mind focused on the fifty other things I should be doing? How many times had I hastily kissed my children and my husband good-bye with the intention of staying on schedule rather than really connecting with them?

This was indeed Lesson #3: *There is something very inauthentic and ill-focused about striving for balance merely so we can keep up with the whirlwind. In the end, it's just an illusion of control.* Where is the joy in all this striving? Where is the calm that all this order is supposed to bring? Isn't that the whole point of life balance? Yup, I decided it was time to say good-bye to this thing called balance.

I returned home from our trip with the intention of putting my lessons from Cuba into effect. And here I am, all these years later, a recovering juggler. Like most recovery processes, I am still learning and very often take it one day at a time. This kind of change doesn't happen overnight. Over the last few years, however, I have gleaned a lot of wisdom as I have learned to let go of that fraudulent, neurotic kind of balance in my life. In its place I have found four ingredients that make for a calmer, happier, more effortless way of living, ingredients I know are fundamental to being the Moms and women we're meant to be: simplicity, flow, intention, and faith. I know they'll do the same for you, too.

> **I'm juggling so hard to keep all the balls in the air that I don't often get to really enjoy what I'm doing.**
>
> —Amy Grant

SIMPLICITY

I was so taken with the simplicity of life in Cuba that upon my return home my first course of action was to start "Project Simplify." This was my pet project to create more simplicity in my life. I instinctively knew that simplicity was a key step in letting go of the complex, frenetic lifestyle I had been living.

True to its name, there was nothing complex or elaborate about Project Simplify. I simply sat down one morning with a pad of paper and started writing down everything I wanted to release from my life, which was basically all the activities, ideas, and possessions that were cluttering up my schedule, my mind, and my home. All this stuff was complicating my life and adding to my need to balance and juggle it all. "The quality of your life is not determined by what you add to it, but by what you take away from it," reminds life coach Cheryl Richardson. I was on a mission to take things away from my life. If it wasn't meeting a basic need or enhancing the quality of my life, it was getting tossed.

Over the next several months I became an expert in what Anne Morrow Lindbergh calls "the art of shedding" in her book *Gift from the Sea*. I learned how little my family and I could actually get along with as we began shedding all the extraneous things from our lives. The questions: *"Is it really necessary?"* and *"What's the trade-off?"* became the driving force behind this process. Firstly, we began shedding physical possessions and clutter. Our unfinished basement was filled with boxes that we hadn't even opened since our move into the house five years earlier. *Is it really necessary?* Clearly not. Gone. We had a ton of baby toys, clothes, and furniture that was being stored away. *Necessary?* Nope. Passed those on to friends and family. Our microwave went on the fritz and we had been talking about replacing it with a new one. *Was it really necessary?* Handy, yes. Necessary, no. We said good-bye to the microwave. (Although I did and still do take a lot of flack for that one.) As we began to purge all these unnecessary items, I began to feel a lightness and freedom I hadn't experienced in a long time. Project Simplify was working.

> **The ability to simplify means to eliminate the unnecessary so that the necessary may speak.**
> —HANS HOFFMAN

The Mommy Diaries

JUST ENOUGH

During the recession, my husband lost his job and we went from a double- to single-income family for an entire year. Talk about a wake up call. While it was difficult and scary, we turned the situation into a valuable learning opportunity as we learned about how much we took for granted and overindulged our family. We learned to live within our means, to buy just enough for what we needed and go without in some cases (which was actually not nearly as bad as one might think), and to be far less wasteful. We also learned to count the many blessings we did have.

When my husband went back to work, we chose not to return to our old ways of living and spending. While some people feel living with just enough means deprivation and going without, we learned that there's far greater value and peace in living simply. I highly recommend it.

Elise, Mom of two and project manager

Next, I tackled calendar clutter and all of the mind clutter that went along with that. At the time, I was involved in *a lot* of activity. Just starting a business, I was part of several weekly and monthly groups for networking and skill-building, not to mention all of the emails, phone calls, and meetings everyday. My daughter had just started school that year and I wanted to be part of the school community, so I volunteered to lead a reading group one morning each week. My son was learning to skate and we had those lessons another morning each week. My daughter took piano lessons one evening each week. And you know all too well how this story goes: on and on and on. We just seemed to be increasingly on-the-go, moving from one activity to the next. Life was full, but not in a just right, satisfied kind of way. It was more of an overabundant, highly uncomfortable, I'm finding it hard to breathe kind of full, I now realized. How had I let my life get this crazy?

There's an expression that spiritual teacher Iyanla Vanzant often uses that goes: *When you see crazy coming, cross the street.* Makes good sense, right? It would seem very applicable to the notion of calendar chaos. The problem for us Moms today is that we know crazy! She's guised in the form of Übermom. She looks just like our mother and our friends and neighbors. She acts like the Moms we see in the media. We see her coming and we say, "Hey! I know you. Let's do lunch." We have grown so accustomed to this ambitious, frenetic kind of lifestyle that all the madness just seems normal to us. This perception makes it difficult and even counter-intuitive to let go of things that seem natural and integral to our lives. But I know that if we pause long enough to ask the questions, as tough as they are, and examine the trade-offs we're making, we'll realize how inefficient we actually are and that we can accomplish much more with much less.

In fact, in his book, *The Myth of Multitasking*, business coach Dave Crenshaw points out how our attempts to "do it all" actually get less done. What we are really doing in our multitasking efforts throughout the day is "switchtasking," or what I call "hypertasking"—jumping

Multitasking: screwing up everything simultaneously.

—Anonymous

around quickly and mindlessly from task to task to task. While hypertasking works for activities requiring less attention such as folding laundry and making the beds while you talk on the phone, it becomes very ineffective for activities requiring more attention and focus. For example, listening to your husband's plans for the weekend while you check your email or driving the carpool while eating a quick meal and trying to find out about your kids' day and their homework for that night.

What happens when we hypertask is that many tasks end up taking longer, mostly because we miss details then make mistakes and have to repeat things. Our stress levels increase because of the frenetic nature of what we're doing. We're more tired because of the extra energy required to move quickly from task to task. And our relationships suffer because we are disconnected and the people around us feel less important because of the lack of attention we are able to give. Those are some pretty serious trade-offs for "getting it all done."

Crenshaw's primary rule on multitasking is this: *The more responsibility you have, the more hats you wear, the more likely you are to become inefficient.* As Moms who wear a multitude of hats everyday, this rule leaves us in a particularly precarious position. It just means that the corollary of this theory must also be true: If more busyness leads to less efficiency, then more simplicity leads to greater effectiveness, a.k.a., less running on empty.

Cut back to Project Simplify . . .

I was determined to simplify my life by letting go of activities that were no longer serving me or were creating too much of a trade-off in my life. All the networking and skill-building activities? Yes, they were important to my business but not necessary in the amount I was committing. The trade-off was taking its toll. I pared those down significantly. I also decided to be less addicted to email, checking it only at regular intervals throughout the day. That proved to be brilliant. Volunteering at my daughter's school? That was also important to me, but again, I realized I could do it in smaller, less time-committing ways. And then there were activities I had committed to because they seemed like the right thing to do—*should's* that became *have to's*. Gah! I let those go, too.

Slowly, my to-do list began to shrink and my life opened up in ways I could never have imagined—more time for nothing doing and connection with my self and family, less stress, more present-moment being, less running on empty, more contentedness, and more serenity. I started becoming more of who I wanted to be, and know I was meant to be.

What started out as a simple project has become a way of life in our family. As our children have gotten older, it has become more challenging to keep life simple. But I always find that the key lies in two things: One, the truth that we cannot do ten things nearly as well as we

If I screw up raising my kids, nothing I achieve will matter much.

—Steve Martin in *Cheaper by the Dozen*

can do three or four things. We just can't. Our job is to choose the three or four things we want to do well at any given time and show up fully for those things. For me, motherhood and family is one of the things I am not willing to half-ass. And two, not getting caught up in making excuses about why you *should* or *have to* be doing something or how you don't have time to simplify. If you focus on making choices instead of excuses by coming back to the questions: *"Is it really necessary?"* and *"What is the trade-off?"* you open up a whole lot of space in your life for being the Mom and woman you're meant to be.

"A wise life is a simple life," say the sages of past and present. This I know for sure.

Reinvention Practice

CREATING WHITE SPACE

Having worked with many graphic designers over the years, I have come to love the concept of "white space." White space is the space in a design that is not merely blank space, but a crucial element that allows for clarity, balance, and emphasis on what's most important. A page that is crammed with text and graphics with little white space leaves the viewer feeling overwhelmed and uncertain as to where to focus her attention.

White space can be used in the design of our lives as well. We can let go of the unnecessary clutter that overwhelms us and prevents us from tuning in to what's really important. Where in your life can you create more "white space"? Where can you remove the non-essentials from your life, home, workday, and calendar to leave the essentials with space around them?

Start small in just one area of your life and start creating pockets of white space. Identify what's least important and slowly remove these non-essential items. Feel the clarity and breathing room you create as the white space unfolds.

FLOW

In addition to simplicity, I also committed to exploring the idea of flow and how I might experience more of that naturalness in my own life. It occurred to me that when we're running around at Mach 10 doing all the juggling we do, we want and need our lives to unfold as smoothly as possible so we can cope. We think that if we find the right balance between all the pieces, things should align the right way and life will be under control—kind of like the juggling trapeze artist at the circus. Home, children, marriage, errands, career, carpools, activities, self—we run a tight rope daily trying to keep all the balls in the air with much angst about dropping any of them. A little to the left . . . a little more to the right . . . steady.

In reality, life doesn't work this way. It doesn't unfold on an even keel and it can't be perfectly arranged how and when we want it. Just like the rest of the natural world, there are always ebbs and flows. There are cycles and seasons that continually unfold as nature maintains its own sense of balance. This is the law of divine order. Our lives are no exception to this natural order of things, especially when it comes to motherhood. When we can recognize and accept that we are not always in control, and that we don't have to be, we can learn how to loosen our grip on life and roll with the natural flow of things.

> **I really feel like life will dictate itself. . . . Allow it to unfold as naturally as possible. Go with the flow. . . . That's the way I've always lived my life.**
>
> —Shania Twain

A Time for Everything

One of the lessons nature and divine order teaches us is that there is a natural rhythm and timing for everything. Days turn into nights. The cold, stillness of winter gives way to the warmth and joyful change of spring. Our hearts beat to a rhythm. The rhythm and timing of our monthly hormone cycles gives us the potential to create new life. Our growth as human beings is centered on a rhythm of timing and development. There is a time and season for everything.

This divine timing applies to our lives as Moms and women, too. There is a season for sleep deprived nights and diapers and cleaning tushies. That doesn't mean there won't be a time for a little black dress and a romantic evening with your husband. In the same way, there's a season for making lunches, helping with homework, and driving to soccer games and piano lessons. That doesn't mean there won't be a season for starting a business or fulfilling your dream to write a novel. There's a time for ambition and a time for stillness; a time for messiness and a time for tidiness; a time for joy and laughter and a time for sadness and tears. In allowing ourselves to embrace this ebb and flow of life rather than trying to circumvent and control it with our own notion of balance and getting-it-all-done-ness, we begin to experience life in a much fuller, more effortless way.

> **We must let go of the life we have planned, so as to accept the one that is waiting for us.**
>
> —Joseph Campbell

Think about it. How can you really know the joys of motherhood if you've never experienced the lows—the exhaustion, frustration, worries, and failures of it? How can you know the thrill of achieving something if you haven't also felt the struggle and loss of something? The brilliance and fullness of life is all in the ebbs and flows, the ups and downs. When we try to manage life so that it unfolds on an even keel, we not only cut ourselves off from experiencing this fullness, but we also create a lot of tension for ourselves and our families by fighting the natural rhythm of life.

Pulitzer Prize-winning journalist and bestselling author Anna Quindlen points out that "You probably can have it all, just not all at the same time. And . . . you might have to make certain compromises when your children are small. But your children are going to be small for a short period of time . . . it will go by in the blink of an eye." We have to let go of this notion of doing it all and having it all at once. We cannot have a picture-perfect home, a strong marriage, raise happy, confident, secure children, be fit and have time for self, and work fifty-hour weeks. As we've already learned, this is a hypertasking approach to life and there will be physical, emotional, and/or spiritual trade-offs. Something's gotta give and we will end up running on empty in one form or another.

> **You can't ride two horses with one ass, Sugarbean.**
> —EARL SMOOTER in *Sweet Home Alabama*

The lesson here is learning to wait and "sit with wanting." This is a BIG shift in the multitasking, do it all, übermom world we live in. We are accustomed to convenience and getting things when we want them. We get frustrated, discouraged, and even angry when we have to wait for things, whether it's waiting in line at the supermarket or waiting for recognition at work or waiting for our children to pick up the pace so we can get out the door. We are rarely fans of waiting.

But there is much opportunity to be found in waiting. Waiting can allow for periods of growth and insight that lead to something better. It can teach us the art of patience. And it can keep us in a place we are meant to be . . . for now. As challenging and uncomfortable as waiting can be, it may be exactly what we need in order to prepare for the next season of our lives.

In her book, *When the Heart Waits*, Sue Monk Kidd offers us these beautiful words, "I hope you'll hear what I'm about to tell you. I hope you'll hear it all the way down to your toes. When you're waiting, you're *not* doing nothing. You're doing the most important something there is. You're allowing your soul to grow up. If you can't be still and wait, you can't become what God created you to be."

> **Real patience requires the willingness to let life unfold at its own pace and reveal itself to you.**
> —JOAN BORYSENKO

Where in your life can you embrace waiting for something you really want? What can you put on hold and stop trying to change, push, or control right now to allow for bigger, more important things to happen? If it's meant to be in the natural order of things, rest assured that the season will come back around.

The Mommy Diaries

WHEN THE TIME IS RIGHT

There's a constant tension that comes with being a mom and also being career driven. A reality television show called last week to invite me to be a participant on their new series. This was a huge opportunity for me and would have meant big things for my business. But my son is only four months old and I just couldn't commit to the grueling production schedule.

In the end, I declined the opportunity. I was incredibly disappointed and many friends and family members thought I was crazy. But in my heart, I knew it was the right thing to do. I was proud that I didn't let my ambition become more important than my family. And, I trust the timing of the Universe. I am doing what feels right for my family and when the time is right, windows will open for "career mom" to do her thing.

Olivia, Mom of two and entrepreneur

The Art of Flexibility

In addition to teaching us about timing and rhythm, nature also teaches us about flexibility—our adaptability and ability to bend without breaking. Living things, in order to thrive and survive, must have an element of flexibility and softness about them otherwise they would be too brittle and weak to endure. The spiritual master Lao-tzu points this out in Verse 76 of his classic text the *Tao Te Ching* (which translated means the "The Book of the Great Way"). He says:

> *All things, including the grass and trees,*
> *are soft and pliable in life;*
> *dry and brittle in death.*
> ....

Kelly Pryde, Ph.D.

> *A tree that cannot bend*
> *will crack in the wind.*

> *The hard and stiff will be broken;*
> *the soft and supple will prevail.*
> (Translation by Wayne W. Dyer, *Living the Wisdom of the Tao*)

There is a lot of wisdom in this notion for us as Moms and women. While we certainly need routines, structure, and schedules to keep our lives on track, if we become too rigid in this need for structure, if we hold on too tight to our expectations and what we think *should be* (e.g., organic juice only, everything in its place, make senior director by age forty, university education is a must), we set ourselves up to crack.

There is good reason for the term "stickler"! Consider how many times you've caught yourself being a stickler about rules and structure with your children, doling out a constant barrage of no's and directives: don't touch that; sit down; drink your milk; do up your coat; no, you can't do that; use your manners; ask for help; no, not right now. We must be pretty tough to take sometimes! Our need for things to unfold according to our shoulds keeps us stuck in a rigid micromanagement mode and life becomes hard to endure, for everyone.

> **Why are you so sure that your micromanagement of every moment in this whole world is so essential? Why don't you let it be?**
>
> —RICHARD FROM TEXAS, *Eat, Pray, Love*

A similar thing happens when we get too caught up in our ambition and strive to "go hard" and "never give up." We push for things and try to control the flow according to what we want, when we want it. But there are no assurances in life—it happens the way it happens. If we are unwilling to soften and bend to the reality around us, we become hard, brittle, and susceptible to breakage. Nature bends and flows with *what is*. It doesn't blow where the wind may take it, but it is flexible and amenable to what arises. This is the only way it can survive.

As counterintuitive as being soft and yielding may seem to us, there is great wisdom and strength to be found in approaching life with this kind of flexibility. The more we are willing to loosen our grip on what we think *should be* and let go of trying to control how our lives unfold, the less resistance we'll encounter and the more effortless life will flow.

An Inflexible Mind

FIVE SIGNS YOU'RE FIGHTING WHAT IS

When you're running on empty and too busy doing, it's easy to get caught up in inflexible thinking. If you find yourself doing any of the following, you have entered the realm of rigid, inflexibility . . .

1. You get stuck in repeating the same thought or behavior that doesn't work and convince yourself that "You like being this way."
2. You're shoulding all over yourself and other people.
3. You're in micromanagement mode, doling out excessive no's and directives and needing things to be "your way or the highway."
4. You're stuck in pissosity, blame, and chronic complaint.
5. You're playing the "There is better than here" game: Things will get better once I _____ (have more money, have more time, get more help, etc.).

The reinvention practice below, "Shifting Focus," will help you turnaround your inflexible thoughts to something more productive and effortless for yourself and your family.

Sometimes being flexible simply means learning to live with a little mess and disorder and letting go of our need to have everything tickety-boo. Sometimes it means learning from mistakes we've made and changing the way we do things. And other times being flexible means letting go of something that we were once really committed to but that no longer seems to fit with our current life situation, as difficult as that may be. There are often no easy answers or decisions when it comes to life and motherhood. But I know that if we do what feels right and are willing to roll with things as they unfold, the way they are meant to, life flows a whole lot smoother.

> **I'm eighteen years behind in my ironing. There's no use doing it now, it doesn't fit anybody I know.**
>
> —PHYLLIS DILLER

Reinvention Practice

SHIFTING FOCUS

Take a look at the inflexible thoughts you have. For example: "I need to put myself first," "Working outside the home is wrong," "There's never enough time," "I need an MBA to be more successful," "My husband never helps out around the house," "Being a stay-at-home Mom is impossible for me." Then for each thought ask yourself the following questions . . .

- Is this 100% undeniably true?
- How do I feel when I believe this thought?
- What are 3 ways my life would change if I let go of this thought and considered the opposite?

Here's an example for the thought: "There's never enough time."

- **Is this 100% undeniably true?** No. We all get 24 hours in each day and some people manage to get things done.
- **How do I feel when I believe this thought?** Stressed out. Frustrated. Tired. Guilty about not managing my time better.
- **What are 3 ways my life would change if I let go of this thought and embraced the opposite?** The opposite of this thought is: "There is enough time." I would feel lighter, that I could breathe easier. I would have more patience and put less pressure on my kids to hurry up. I would sleep better at night.

In being more flexible and considering alternative thoughts and possibilities in this way, we open ourselves up to a calmer and more effortless—a more natural—approach to living.

Source: Katie, B. (2003). Loving What Is. *New York: Three Rivers Press.*

INTENTION

Part of my juggling recovery process was struggling with the idea of embracing the natural flow of things versus letting life just passively happen. Like the rest of my generation, I had grown up with the notion that goals were crucial to achievement. We need S.M.A.R.T. (specific, measurable, attainable, results-oriented, and time-focused) goals and a clear vision in order to be successful, right? Was I supposed to just let all of that go and allow things to unfold as they may? That felt loosey-goosey to me, like living life completely by default. I also knew, however, that the overly ambitious, go hard, single-focused kind of goal-setting that I was accustomed to was not the answer either. That was like putting blinders on and missing out on all the good things around you while you worked your butt off chasing something you *hoped* would happen in the future. No thanks.

But what was the in-between? After much reflection and trial-and-error, here's the realization I came to: Letting go and living in flow doesn't mean we live aimlessly or say, "Oh look, an obstacle. I'd better stop or change direction." It means being clear about our intention—knowing *what* we want and *why* we want it—and committing to that intention with both action and the confidence that we can change direction when it makes sense. This is called living an intentional life.

Living an intentional life is predicated on two things: values and choice. Our values are connected to the inner compass we began establishing in the fourth pathway on YOU and choice is the conscious selection of acting on those values—what we deem is most desirable, admirable, and honorable—given our options. Let's take a closer look at each . . .

Values

More than a prioritized checklist of what's important to us, our values are part of our inner compass that guide how we live. One of my biggest pet peeves is when you ask a person or group a question about why they're doing something and they say, "Well that's the way it's always been done." We hear something similar when we ask our kids why they did something they weren't supposed to. They say, "Jimmy told me to." Or "She did it first!" There's simply no thought or conscious intent behind the actions, they just get caught up in what's going on around them. The same thing happens all too often with us as Moms—we get caught up in ways. Maybe our parents expected things a certain way, maybe we're following in an older sibling's footsteps, or maybe our fellow Moms do a certain thing. And sometimes, just like our kids, we do things "because the experts told us to." We get caught up in ways, expectations, and shoulds and rarely do we ask ourselves, "What do *I* want?" and "What's important to me?"

> **Would you stop thinking about what everyone wants? Stop thinking about what I want, what he wants, what your parents want. What do YOU want? What do you WANT?**
>
> —NOAH CALHOUN in *The Notebook*

Start asking yourself intentional, values-based questions: What do I want for myself, my children, my marriage, my family? What is most important to me in the grand scheme of things? What does success really mean to me? What does it mean to be a mother, a wife, a woman? Why am I doing this? Am I doing this out of fear of not being enough or out of love and what I know is right for me and my family? Until you get clear about what you want and why, you will continue to either live by default or get caught up in somebody else's way. Know what YOU want, why you want it, and do it on purpose.

Reinvention Practice

DEFINING SUCCESS: A TALE OF TWO MOMS

Many of us get caught up in the quest for success for ourselves and our children without ever defining what it means to us. The following story adapted from Mark Albion's "The Good Life Parable" highlights the importance of being in tune with how we define success . . .

The owner/CEO of a successful company was on a weekend getaway with her family in a small Mennonite village when she came across a woman selling fresh baked goods.

The CEO bought some of the woman's baking for herself and her children and was amazed at how fresh and delicious it was. Even her children said it was the best they'd ever had. Curious, the CEO asked the Mennonite woman how much baking she sold in a day. "Oh, I only sell them for a couple of hours," the woman replied with a smile. The CEO asked why she didn't set up for longer and sell more.

The woman smiled again and said, "In two hours, I sell enough to help support my family's needs." The CEO was perplexed and had to ask, "But what do you do with the rest of your time?"

The woman replied, "In the morning, I spend time with my children, do some baking and come here to sell my goods. In the afternoon, I tend to my garden, enjoy a relaxing dinner with my family, then help my children with their homework before we gather in the village each evening to spend time with family and friends. My days are quite full."

The CEO scoffed, "I have an MBA and I can help you. If you baked more goods and spent the day selling them, you could make enough money to open your own bakery. You could hire more people to help you and then brand your baking and package it to sell to large retail stores. After that, you could expand even more by opening small retail outlets at major malls."

The CEO went on to add, "You would need to travel and spend more time in the city in order to network, partner, and grow your company. You'd probably get asked to do interviews and talk to other women about running a business. You could even write a book! You would be very successful."

"Really? How long will all this take?" the woman asked.

"Probably between 10 and 15 years," the CEO explained.

"But what will I do then?" asked the Mennonite.

The CEO laughed and said, "That's the best part. When the time is right you could sell your company and become very rich. You could make millions."

"Millions?" the woman asked. "But then what?"

The CEO was a bit stumped, but then replied, "Well, I guess you would retire. You could move to a small quiet community where you would have plenty of time for your family and friends. You could bake, garden, and have dinner with your husband and children every evening. You would have a very contented life."

*   *   *   *   *

Know what success means to you—what you want and why you want it—otherwise you could climb all the rungs of the ladder to success only to find your ladder is up against the wrong wall. Anna Quindlen reminds us, "If your success is not on your own terms, if it looks good to the world but does not feel good in your heart, it is not success at all."

Source: Adapted from "The Good Life Parable" by Mark Albion in More Than Money. *San Francisco: BK Life, 2008; and "The Good Life" video by Mark Albion. Oakland: Free Range Studios, 2008. Adapted with permission.*

Choice

Once we get clear about our values and intentions, we must make choices in order to live them. Making choices for ourselves is one thing, but when we're in the business of people-making and responsible for the lives of our children, choice takes on a whole new meaning. In fact, the choices we are called to make as Moms and women can sometimes feel downright impossible. Making choices that are aligned with our deepest values and intentions as both Moms and women often means change—sometimes BIG change—and that can be scary. And then we worry, too, about making the wrong choices: What if I fail? What if I screw up my kids? What if I can't pay my bills? What if I regret *not* doing this? But not choosing because we are afraid of change or because it's hard and uncertain does not change the reality of what is. It simply means we will continue to live out of alignment with what we truly want and believe in. And as I've said before, denying or ignoring what we know to be true and fighting change is how we betray ourselves. It's like sweeping our hearts and souls under a rug, moment by moment, day by day.

Let's consider some of the big choices we grapple with as Moms and women: Should I go back to work or stay at home? Can I afford to stay home? Do we choose daycare or homecare? What about a nanny? Should I start my own business? Can I work part-time? Can I take a few years off and expect to get hired again? These are not easy questions and there are no straightforward answers. The only thing we can do is make the best choice with what we value, what we know, and what is true for us in that moment. The choice that works today may not be what works tomorrow or it may turn out to work better than we could have imagined. There are no guarantees. All I know for sure is that if you make conscious choices that are aligned with your inner compass—who you are and what you value—you're choosing to grow and become more of who you are meant to be.

> **I think if you love what you do, and you love the choices you've made in your life, somehow that drives you forward to enjoy it all. Even the chaos, even the exhaustion of it, and even when it seems out of balance.**
> —ANGELINA JOLIE

The beauty of intention and choice is that you won't feel like you are sacrificing. You'll never wonder with regret "*What if?*" You'll stop concerning yourself with what others think of you. And you'll have the confidence and courage to make new choices as you see fit. In this way, you can never make the wrong choice. How's that for some reinvention?!

And in the event that you know in your heart you want something different but can't choose it right now, remember that there is a time for everything. Delay doesn't mean denial. Hold on to your intention and wait until the time is right. Oh yeah, and try a little faith . . .

What's All the Fuss?

THE STAY-AT-HOME VS. CAREER DEBATE

It's the age-old debate: stay at home and raise your family vs. have a family and a career. Discussions and debates over women, motherhood, and career have been going on for decades and are fraught with controversy and contradiction. So who's right? You are.

Decisions around careers, daycares, nannies, and staying home are highly personal—you have to do what works for you and your family. What's most important is that you are in tune with the needs of your children, your home, and your Self and that you allow the decision to pass through your heart rather than be dictated by your ego. The ego will always coax you with: "You've worked so hard for this. Why would you give it up?" "Good Moms stay home." "What about that new kitchen you want?"

Bickering between stay-at-home Moms and working Moms merely reflects our insecurities, fears, and thoughts of not being enough or having enough. Until we do the work of reinvention, until we get rid of all the emotional clutter, get clear about who we are and what really matters to us, and make choices based on that clarity, we will never be happy with what we have. The grass will always be greener on the other side.

When you know who you are and what's important to you and you love the choices you've made, that will give you the confidence to enjoy it all, even through all the uncertainties and imbalances of it.

FAITH

Remember when you were pregnant and for nine months you waited patiently for Mother Nature to do its thing and grow your baby in the perfect way it knows how? You ate healthy, exercised, and rested, but other than that you waited . . . and trusted. You trusted that nature would give your baby two eyes and a nose and ten little fingers, exactly where they're supposed to be. This is called faith—turning things over to and trusting in a force greater than yourself to handle life. And the truth is that many aspects of our lives, and our children's lives, are handled by that same force.

God, Goddess, Divine, Yahweh, Allah, Universe, Source, whatever you choose to call it, there's no denying

Life's funny like that, once you let go of the wheel, you might end up right where you belong.

—BRITTANY MURPHY in *Little Black Book*

that this all-pervasive, all-knowing force exists. Our struggles lie in trying to take over for that force, thinking we know better, and trying to control things on our own terms. It's true. Even when our children are born, we say, "Thank you, God. You've created absolute perfection in this little baby . . . but we'll take over from here." Faith is not a convenient, practice-it-when-I-need-it kind of thing. It's an all the time thing. Whether we realize it or not, we are always in a state of faith and trust for many things: going to bed each night without worrying about waking up in the morning, the healing of a cut, breathing, the rising and setting of the sun each day. When we can extend this faith to other areas of our lives, then we really begin to practice the art of letting go. We'll trust that our children will learn to walk, talk, read, write, and find their way in life without excessive pushing and prodding from us. We'll trust that our decisions and choices about life, family, marriage, self, and motherhood will work out and unfold the way they need to. And we'll trust that we will always have everything we need to deal with whatever life brings our way—the ups and downs, highs and lows, and ebbs and flows of it all.

The Mommy Diaries

SERENITY NOW

At fifty-five years of age with three grown children, I still have to remind myself that I am not in control of their lives. I want to help them and save them from making mistakes and getting hurt, but they will learn what they need to in the way they choose to learn it. I have learned that my job is to step aside and let them make their choices while keeping my arms extended should they need a helping hand or a hug. I've also learned that "The Serenity Prayer" is a great friend: *God, grant me the serenity to accept the things I cannot change, the courage to change the things I can and the wisdom to know the difference.* That's gotten me through a lot of challenging times as a mother!

Georgina, Mom of three, Grandma of two, and retail manager

Let go. Say good-bye to that ill-focused kind of balance we've adopted with all of its struggling and striving and stress. Let. It. Go. And when you have simplified, practiced patience and flexibility, intended, made conscious choices, worked hard, and given and tried and hoped . . . have faith. Some things might not work out the way you think they should or in the timeframe you want, but they will flow exactly the way

When you have done all that you can do, give it up to that thing that is greater than yourself and let it become part of the flow.

—OPRAH WINFREY

they are meant to. Even better, you'll experience a level of serenity and joy in your life that can only be found in this perfectly lopsided world called motherhood.

*   *   *   *   *

In her book *The Call,* poet and author Oriah Mountain Dreamer offers us these words of wisdom on the art of letting go:

> When we let go of wanting things to be a certain way, when we let go of our certainty that we know how things should be, we find ourselves letting go of resisting or resenting what is true in this moment, truly at peace with what is often an unpredictable and sometimes messy human life. And in this acceptance we . . . [come] into alignment with what is . . . with that flow of life. Of course the flow of life . . . may set you down someplace you could not have imagined. And in every situation, no matter what options life presents you, the choice about how to be where you are—here—remains yours. (81-82)

REFLECTION AND ACTION FOR PATH SIX

✄ Consider starting a simplicity project of your own. What things in your life can you let go of today or at least set the intention to let go of when the time is right? Physical possessions? A commitment that has become a "should" or "have to"? A relationship that is draining you? A job or career decision that no longer fits with your current life situation? Overscheduled activities for your children? Challenge yourself to let go of *more* than feels comfortable. Notice how you feel as you begin to create this kind of "white space" in your life.

✄ In what ways are you trying to control or fight *what is* in your life or your children's lives? Do you have rigid ideas or goals for what *should be* (e.g., make senior director by age forty; my children must go to university; my husband should be contributing to at least fifty percent of the work at home)? Do you get hung up on doing certain things because they are expected by others or because the experts told you to? Are you trying to do it all and be it all at the same time? What options or possibilities does the reinvention practice, "Shifting Focus" present to you for letting go and becoming more flexible?

✄ In your journal, write down your thoughts on the intentional, values-based questions described in the section "Values." Identify what YOU want and why you want it as well as whether or not your life is aligned with these values. It sometimes helps to identify what you want with the end in mind. Commonly expressed regrets amongst the dying are powerful lessons in choosing to live a life in alignment with what matters most: loving more, working less, worrying less, being true to oneself, and choosing more happiness. "It's never too late to be what you might have been," wrote the English novelist George Eliot. The choice about how to be here in this life as a Mom and woman is yours.

FURTHER READING FOR PATH SIX

The Call: Discovering Why You Are Here by Oriah Mountain Dreamer (New York: HarperCollins, 2003)

Oriah gently guides readers on her journey of discovering and heeding her own call of what it means to live fully and deeply in the world. Through her struggles and insights, readers are given the opportunity to discover and embrace the essence of who they truly are.

Daring Greatly: How the Courage to be Vulnerable Transforms the Way We Live, Love, Parent, and Lead by Brené Brown (New York: Gotham Books, 2012)

Researcher and thought leader, Dr. Brené Brown, challenges us to re-think what we know about vulnerability. Based on twelve years of research, she argues that vulnerability is not weakness, but rather our clearest path to courage, engagement, and meaningful connection.

The Rhythm of Life: Living Every Day With Passion and Purpose by Matthew Kelly (New York: Fireside, 2005)

This book offers inspiring and practical strategies for cutting through the stifling clutter of everyday life to living out loud and on purpose. Kelly helps readers discover their deepest longings in order to live with more happiness, health, compassion, and purpose.

Loving What Is: Four Questions that Can Change Your Life by Byron Katie (New York: Three Rivers Press, 2003)

Katie outlines the four-step inquiry process that turned around her ten-year downward spiral of rage, paranoia, and depression. The process gives readers the opportunity to challenge and free themselves from their own thoughts and beliefs that lead to emotional suffering.

PATH 7

THE ULTIMATE REALIZATION

Remembering Why You Are Here

It's 8:55 A.M. on a Monday morning. The sun is shining and I am standing in the school playground helping my daughter put on her backpack as we wait for the school bell to ring. I give her a big hug and wish her a great day at school, and just as she's about to walk off, she turns to me and says in her sweet matter-of-fact voice (the one that leads my Dad to call her "the professor"), "I only have two things to remember today." "What's that, honey?" I ask. "One," as she looks down at her little hand and holds out one finger, "is that I'm going to see you really soon . . . in just a few hours." "And two," as she holds out a second finger, "is that I love you." As my heart starts melting right there on the playground, I can't help but be equally blown away by the assuredness and commonsensical manner with which she says these things. At six years old, she has the simple knowing that we all forget and spend our lifetimes trying to figure out: At the end of the day, making the choice to love in our unique way is what it's all about.

We come into this world designed perfectly to love and be who we were meant to be. Perfectly and unconditionally. You only have to be at the receiving end of a toddler's soggy cookie or notice your baby's joyful smile when you greet him at his crib in the morning to see that we are born in a perfect state of love. By "love" I don't mean sentimental, gushy, lets-sit-around-and-sing-kumbaya love. What I'm referring to here is a state of being that is open, gentle, non-judgmental, giving, joyful, and present. This is our natural state of being early on in life. And then we forget.

As we develop and go through life, we are taught and exposed to ideas and experiences that contradict our natural state of love. All the things we've explored up to this point—the whirlwind of motherhood; our rational, do-it-all, left-brain lifestyle; emotional clutter; disconnection from Self; disenchantment; etc—are what shift us away from this natural tendency to love. They

> **The truth doesn't stop being the truth just because we're not looking at it. Love merely becomes clouded over, or surrounded by mental mists.**
>
> —MARIANNE WILLIAMSON

create blockages and barriers to love and keep us stuck in an unnatural state of running on empty. The process of reinvention has been all about removing those blockages and shifting us back to our natural tendency to love.

This remembering is especially important to us as Moms. Our female biology combined with our natural tendency to love affords us the ability to nurture, heal, teach, and, above all else, to give. Our children rely on us for these forms of love. And while most of us feel that we are constantly giving, doing for others from a state of running on empty is not the same as loving and giving. It is, in fact, sacrificing. Running on empty and sacrificing for our children and our families comes from a place of lack and does not feel good to anyone. Real loving and giving, on the other hand, comes from a place of generosity and an open heart and is one of the most joyous things we can do—for ourselves, for our children, and for everyone around us. It is why we are here and the ultimate realization in becoming the Moms and women we are meant to be.

In an essay written in *Handbook for the Heart,* physician and bestselling author Bernie Siegel writes, "*We're here to learn to love more fully. That is the meaning and reason behind our lives. Each of us has a choice about how to love . . . in our unique way.*" This pathway is all about this one simple truth that we will continue to come back to time and time again throughout our lifetimes. I call it the art of loving and it really is the meaning and purpose behind our lives. You're already on your way to reconnecting with feeling and your feminine wisdom. You're restoring your "fizziology" and removing emotional clutter. You're rediscovering YOU, enchantment, and how to let go of the need to do it all and get it all done. It's now time to remember why you are here and choose how to be in this life.

That is the ultimate realization: A departure from the hurried fogginess of doing, sacrificing, and running on empty. A shift in focus. A return to love.

The one eternal question for us all is *how better can we love.*

—HENRY DRUMMOND

THE ART OF LOVING

Prior to embarking on this leg of the reinvention journey, I had often heard the sayings: "If you just love your children, that is enough" and "Love is all you need." I remember thinking they were somewhat cliché, maybe even a bit Pollyanna. Don't get me wrong. At the time, I firmly believed that love is an essential ingredient to a full and happy life. It's just that these phrases seemed to be a bit simplistic. Of course I love my children and my family—not a day goes by that I don't tell them how much I love them. But I felt there was a whole lot more to raising children and being a Mom and woman than love alone. What about teaching our children about problem-solving, learning right from wrong, developing emotional intelligence and social skills? What about education, sports, art, and music? Surely these things are vital to their development as well, aren't they? And what about our own needs as women to discover our passions and strengths and make a contribution to the world? It seemed to me that love alone was not the complete package.

It wasn't until I came across a beautiful little book by renowned Zen monk Thich Nhat Hanh called *True Love* that I discovered I had been thinking about love and these simple phrases all wrong. All this time I had been thinking about love as a noun—a feeling of love, rather than as a verb— an act that is infused with love. While one is an emotional experience, the other is an intentional practice, and that subtle difference led to a big change in my thinking, and my actions. With this discovery, the seventh pathway began to unfold.

In my own experience and my observations of other families, it occurred to me how often we go through our days on automatic pilot. We get up, we get everyone dressed and ready for the day, we say "I love you" in passing on our way out the door, we make meals, we help with homework, we tidy and clean, we get everyone ready for bed, etc, etc. And then we get up the next day to do it all over again. If we're really honest with ourselves, how often do we go about all of these daily routines and activities with loving intentions? Yes we do all these things because we love our children and our family, but we don't always do them in a loving way. That little piece of intention makes all the difference.

Life on automatic pilot leads to love on automatic pilot, or what I call *rote love*—loving in a way that is habitual, without thought and attention to the meaning behind our actions. It seems many of us today are living in this state of rote love. It's no wonder so many of us feel the sense that something is missing in our lives. In *True Love*, Thich Nhat Hanh points out that the art of loving in a real way requires thought, intention, and practice; it doesn't just magically happen. In other words, we have to work at it. So how do we go about this practice? How do we work at infusing love into our everyday acts?

There are three practices we can engage in to develop the art of loving: attention, acceptance, and appreciation. Why these three specifically? Because at our deepest level of being, we all have the same profound need: *We all need to feel seen, heard, understood and appreciated. We each need to know that we matter simply because we are here.* As much as our children need us to provide them with the basic physical necessities for survival—food, water, clothing, and shelter—they also need us to provide them with this most basic emotional and spiritual necessity. This is an essential element of loving and caring for our children as well as being the Moms and women we're meant to be. When we practice attention, acceptance, and appreciation we meet that deep emotional and spiritual need, not only for our children and our partner, but also for everyone around us. This is how we bring more love into our lives on a day-to-day basis. This is the art of true loving.

> At the deepest level, it's real love and care that people crave. Give those things, and . . . you'll truly make your mark on the world.
>
> —Doc Childre and Howard Martin

Love through the Stages

HOW LOVE CHANGES
THROUGH THE STAGES OF RELATIONSHIPS

"All beginnings are lovely," says a French proverb. This is especially true when it comes to love and relationships. Whether it's romantic love or mother-child love, the first stage of any loving relationship is the **"in love" stage** where hormones and brain chemicals are in overdrive making it very easy for us to be loving, patient, attentive, and affectionate. But as time passes and the chemicals subside, we enter the more effortful second stage of power/ growth struggles.

In the **power/growth struggle stage**, we go through an adjustment period where we struggle to get our needs met. This is when all of our "stuff" surfaces, so depending on the extent of the "junk in your trunk" (emotional baggage, not the other kind!) and how running on empty you are, the extent and severity of this stage will vary. This is where the reinvention work comes in to counter the power struggles, impatience, frustration, anger, and disconnects that can become commonplace. Reinvention practices are key to reaching the third and final stage of a loving relationship—real love.

In the **real love stage**, we are actively developing a strong sense of Self and healing our emotional issues which allows us to be more open, present, vulnerable, and accepting of the other person for who they are, not who we think they should be. While we will continue to cycle through these stages throughout our lives, doing the work of reinvention to reach the real love stage enables us to experience more love, joy, and fulfillment in our relationships.

Attention: Being There With Intention and Mindfulness

Thich Nhat Hanh tells us, "The most precious gift we can offer anyone is our attention." Offering our attention is the ability to be truly present with another person and to listen with our heart and our mind. This kind of listening is a skill that is typically not well developed in most of us. In general, we tend to give our divided attention—we partially listen while we multitask or think about a dozen other things that need to get done. And as we discovered in the previous pathway, this kind of multitasking and divided attention leads us to disconnect from the other person who doesn't feel seen or heard. Because of this, many people today, especially children, are starved for loving attention.

Becoming more fully present with mindfulness and intention in our actions and interactions reflects a generosity of spirit. It says, "You matter and are important enough to me that I want to be fully present with you." One of the ways my husband and I have done this with our children is to have one-on-one dates with each of them from the time they were quite small. We've always found that planning and going on a date with them is very special. They love getting the undivided attention, they behave completely differently, and we connect in positive ways. I remember one particular date with my son when he was about two and a half years old. We were wandering around our local bookstore after having lunch and reading books together when he looked up at me and said, "Mommy and GG still on date?" (His name is Grayson; he used to call himself GG.) When I answered yes, he clapped his hands and with a huge smile on his face shouted, "Yay!" Being there for someone with presence and loving attention is a little thing that creates a lot of meaning and richness in our lives.

Love cannot survive if you just give it scraps of yourself, scraps of your time, scraps of your thoughts.
—MARY O'HARA

There are many easy ways we can practice this kind of loving attention in our daily lives. When we say "I love you," we can look at the person and say the words in a heartfelt way rather than habitually in passing. We can take time to engage in genuine conversation—asking questions and really listening to what is being said. We can be mindful of our thoughts and feelings when tucking our children into bed. We can ask ourselves, "Am I rushing to get onto other tasks or am I fully present and engaged with my child?" When we wake up in the morning, we can set an intentional focus for the day by asking ourselves not what do I have *do* today, but how do I want to *be* today.

Author Robert Johnson calls this kind of mindfulness "stirring the oatmeal." In his book, *We,* he writes, "'Stirring the oatmeal' is a humble act—not exciting or thrilling. But it symbolizes a relatedness that brings love down to earth. It represents a willingness to share ordinary human life, to find meaning in the simple, unromantic tasks: earning a living, living within a budget, putting out the garbage, feeding the baby in the middle of the night." Infusing our daily actions with loving intentions is not always romantic or thrilling, but the attention and presence we bring to our everyday ordinary acts is key to shifting from rote love to real love.

The consciousness of loving and being loved brings a warmth and richness to life that nothing else can bring.
—OSCAR WILDE

Reinvention Practice

THE MINDFUL HUG

Showing affection is an essential element of attention and the art of loving. When we touch someone in a gentle, loving way it says, "You are important to me. I care for you and I will protect you."

Sharing a hug with a loved one is one of the most common and powerful forms of affection we show. In fact, psychologist Virginia Satir once said "We need four hugs a day for survival, eight for maintenance, and twelve for growth." To infuse more love into this simple act, try this beautiful hugging meditation offered by Thich Nhat Hanh the next time you hug your child, husband, or loved one:

> *When you take the person you love in your arms you must practice deeply: "Breathing in I know that you are alive in my arms; breathing out I am very glad."*

Source: Nhat Hanh, Thich (1997). True Love. *Boston: Shambhala Publications.*

Acceptance: Practicing Tolerance and Compassion

Once we are able to be more fully present in our actions and interactions, we can then practice recognizing the presence of the people around us. Recognizing another's presence does not simply mean we notice that the person is there. It means that we really see, hear, *and* understand the person. We tune in and connect with that person. We look deeply in a way that allows us to put ourselves in their shoes. This does not come naturally for most of us. We tend to get wrapped up in all of our daily to-do's and connect with people in a cursory way. We tend to stay stuck in annoyance and frustration with our children, our husband, and other people who irritate us. We tend to cling to our notions of how things *should be* and judge other people when they don't meet those expectations.

> **You are here for a limited time, would you rather spend it being irritated or being loving?**
>
> —Bernie Siegel, M.D.

Yes we have many challenging behaviors and situations to contend with as Moms and women, but our job is to teach our children how to deal with these kinds of frustrations in a constructive way. Responding to challenging behaviors and situations in a tolerant way rather than reacting in an angry, judgmental way is a very loving thing to do for our family.

I learned a valuable lesson in tolerance several years ago when my daughter was about six years old. Our family was just coming off of a two-week vacation, and I was running on empty. In addition to being tired, I had had it with the bickering and tattle-taling between her and her younger brother, the complaining and the whining. And I was tired of repeating myself, over and over and over. As a result, I found myself being very quick to anger and over-reacting to the smallest of things.

As coincidence would have it, my daughter came to me during that time complaining that she was having a recurring bad dream: monsters were chasing our family. When we sat down to talk about the dream, it turned out the monster was actually a giant. A scary girl giant. (You see where this is going, right?!). We looked up the meaning of giants appearing in dreams and here's what it said:

> *"You may be coming to terms with repressed feelings about adults from when you were a child. They may have seemed frightening in some way."*

With tears in her eyes, my daughter confirmed that she found my angry over-reactions scary. *Gulp.* I hugged her and thanked her for telling me about her dream. I told her I was sorry for my behavior and that I was going to work hard to do better. And rather than wallow in the guilt and awful feelings I had, I began thinking about how I was going to put this promise into action, about how I was going to "do better."

As I thought about frustration and intolerance and my over-reactions, I was reminded of a quote from Stephen Covey I had come across years earlier: "Between stimulus and response, there is a space. In that space lies our freedom and power to choose our response. In our response lies our growth and our happiness."

And there it was, plain and simple: Tolerance is a choice.

Amidst all the noise, interruptions, and demands we face on a daily basis, the ability to respond with patience and tolerance is a choice. Is it an easy one? Heck no! As parents we are probably in the most demanding and challenging role when it comes to tolerance and patience. But having signed up for this role, we have both the responsibility and the power to make that choice, not only for the sake of our children, but also for our own growth and happiness.

Reinvention Practice

THE PATIENCE PLAN

Patience is not acquired overnight. It's like building up a muscle—you need to work on it everyday. Here are some strategies for building up your patience muscle:

- **Think patience.** What you focus on is what you create, so find ways to keep patience in your thoughts throughout the day—post quotes on patience around your home and workspace, find a mantra or prayer to recite, make a commitment in the morning to be more loving and tolerant that day.
- **Practice mindfulness.** It is so easy to react and over-react. When we can catch ourselves in those moments where interruptions and minor irritations occur and our instinct is to respond mindlessly with impatience and annoyance, we have the opportunity to find the space where we can . . .
- **Stop, breath, and think to avoid mindless over-reacting.** I've used this technique for years for helping my children deal with their frustration. Turns out it works just as well for us adults! When you feel impatience creeping in, stop and take a breath. This is a simple and powerful little strategy that allows you to approach a situation with more calmness and clarity. As mentioned in Path Three on emotional feng shui, you can even benefit from taking an actual "time out" where you remove yourself from the situation to take some calming breaths and refocus before you respond. Once in that space, you can . . .
- **Change your mind and choose a kinder, more loving response.**

Our presence, acceptance, and compassion are so precious to our families. Practicing tolerance and acceptance means accepting our children, partner, and loved ones for who they are—mistakes, quirks, habits, peccadilloes, and all—instead of who we think they *should be*. It means giving a reminder the twentieth time with the same patience as the first time. It means leaving the crookedly made bed, recognizing that our child did his best to make it well. It means taking the time to listen deeply to our loved ones to truly understand where they are coming from and to just be there for them rather than reacting with a quick fix, judgment, blame, or "I told you so."

Mother Teresa used to say, "If you're busy judging someone, you have no time to love them." These words are very wise because two things cannot occupy the same space at the same time. This is simply a law of physics. In every situation, we are either acting out of fear, anger, and judgment or out of love. That is the choice we are always making whether we intend to or not. As we continue to reinvent ourselves, it becomes much easier to make choices grounded in real love—attentive, accepting, compassionate, unattached-to-our-idea-of-what-should-be kind of love—rather than fear, anger, and judgment.

Reinvention Practice

THE LOVE EXPERIMENT

Making choices and acting in ways that are grounded in real love requires a shift from our rote, everyday ways of reacting to a more compassionate, mindful way of being. Here is an experiment you can try to help you make the shift . . .

For the next several days, or even week, commit to practicing only loving thoughts and actions. During this time, refuse to allow any thoughts of judgment, criticism, blame, or gossip to creep into your mind or escape from your mouth. Think and act only in loving ways in all of your encounters and interactions. Commit to loving thoughts and energy when you wake up in the morning and extend that love wherever you go throughout the day—in making breakfast for your children, to the grouchy co-worker in your office, to the cashier at the supermarket, in greeting your spouse at the end of the day, and even when looking into the mirror. Infuse every moment of this time with only love.

Your ego and your conditioning will resist this task, but if you stick with it for a few days, you will begin to notice a change in yourself and the people around you. You will experience more love, joy, and freedom and less fear, anger, and judgment. You will realize that you have nothing to prove and that all you want and hope for as a Mom and woman is already here. It always was.

Source: Dyer, Wayne W. (1999). Manifest Your Destiny. *New York: HarperPaperbacks.*

As Moms and women, it is also important to recognize that the practice of acceptance, tolerance, and compassion applies just as much to our fellow Moms. I'm always amazed and saddened at how quick many mothers are to judge other mothers. When we attack one another through judgment, gossip, and blame, it is unloving and toxic, not only to the women we attack, but also to our children who are tuned in to everything we do. *We all do the best we can with what we have and what we know at the time.* Let's remember this and practice accepting beliefs and behaviors that may differ from our own. Accepting them doesn't mean you have to agree with them, it simply means you can acknowledge them with an empathetic mind and a compassionate heart. You never know what struggles a fellow Mom may be facing at any given time. As we continue to travel the reinvention pathways, healing our emotional issues and increasing our capacity to care for and love our own selves, we become much better able to extend that love to others in every encounter.

The Mommy Diaries

CLOSE ENCOUNTER OF THE JUDGING KIND

I took my three youngest kids for lunch at the food court in the local mall the other day. My toddler had a meltdown and went into a full, high-pitched scream. Yeah, you know the sound. As I was trying to manage my stressful moment, an elderly woman looked over at us and shook her head in disgust. She then informed me that I should do a better job of "training" my son. I almost had a temper tantrum myself at that point. I asked her to consider that next time she sees an exhausted mother struggling, why not offer to give her a hand? Mrs. McJudgerson was all criticism with nothing helpful to offer.

When the spectacle came to an end and the woman had left, my lip began to quiver. Then came a quiet tear and then another. It occurred to me that this woman is the reason mothers worry that we are doing a bad job. She is the reason mothers get trapped at home, socially isolated, because they are afraid of going out with their small children and being judged.

At the end of the day, I was able to take comfort in one simple fact: this woman is not my mother-in-law. I am eternally grateful for that. Imagine being related to that parenting expert!

Julie Cole, Mom of six and co-founder of Mabel's Labels, Inc.

Source: Adapted from "Mrs. Judgy McJudgerson at the Mall" by Julie Cole (March 1, 2011). YummyMummyClub.ca Blog. Adapted with permission.

Appreciation: Seeing and Honoring Specialness

Both of my children love hearing the story about the day they were born. I tell each about how excited and anxious their Dad and I were for them to arrive and about our trip to the hospital. I tell them about how we cried when they were finally born because we were so happy—we had never been happier in our whole life. And I tell each of them how lucky we were because of all the babies born in the hospital that day, we got the best one.

I can't even put into words the reaction my children have at hearing this story. It's like a brilliant display of happiness, joy, fulfillment, bliss, pride, and love all at once—almost as if they are going to burst at the seams with all the happiness and love they feel in that moment. Why? Because hearing this story in this way makes them feel worthy, significant, and valued. They feel loved and treasured.

In Path Five on re-enchanting your everyday life, we explored the power of gratitude in our daily lives. Appreciation, in the context of this seventh pathway, is slightly different. While it certainly involves recognizing and expressing thanks, appreciation here has more to do with recognizing and honoring the value and worthiness of another person. It says, "You are special and important. I treasure you."

When we're running on empty—tired, overscheduled, and disconnected from our own needs—we begin tuning in to everything that's not working and that we don't like. We start to feel bitter and unappreciated. We complain, nitpick, criticize, and fault-find. As we fail to honor our own value, we fail to honor the value of others. In this state, we have little to give. The good news is that as we begin to restore our inner resources and recognize our own value and worthiness (remember your personal genius from Path Four?), it becomes easier to help others, especially our children and loved ones, feel the inner glow that comes from being appreciated.

From saying "thank you" for little things, to celebrating accomplishments, to recognizing talents, to noticing the way they dress, talk, laugh, share, and style their hair, we can let our loved ones know that we see their specialness and we appreciate them. Even when saying good night to our children, we can say "Good night special girl" and "I

Precious and fragile things need special handling.

—Depeche Mode

love you special boy." The more you reinvent your life, the more you can open your heart and focus on radiating this kind of loving appreciation to the people around you. And as the old saying goes: *The more you give, the more you get.*

Letter to Mom

DEAR MOM: TEN THINGS I NEED MOST

Dear Mom,

I know I often talk back, roll my eyes and tune you out, but here's the thing: I really, really do need you. Sometimes I think you forget that I'm just a kid and that I still have many special needs. So if I was able, here are 10 things I would tell you I need the most . . .

1. Spend time with me and connect with me. It helps me know that I matter. (Not to mention that you are the most important person in my life and I really want to be with you.)
2. Please slow down and take your time with me. I cannot do things at your skill level or on your schedule.
3. Cheer me on and celebrate all of my little successes. It inspires me.
4. Hug me often. It helps me feel loved and special and it's good for my developing brain.
5. Be as patient with me the 20th time you teach me something, as you were the first time. My brain doesn't learn as quickly as yours and I sometimes forget.
6. Please don't raise your voice—I'm not stupid or deaf. I am a child who is still learning and making lots of mistakes. Approach me gently with an open heart.
7. Challenge me but do not push me too hard to progress or achieve. Let me have fun and take pleasure in where I am today.
8. Respect me by speaking to me, not about me to others like I'm not there.
9. Set clear expectations and limits for my behavior. It helps me feel safe.
10. Be the person you want me to be. You are my biggest hero and I want to learn from you how to be in this world.

We all love our children and our families. There's no doubt about that. Maybe we just need to work a little harder at how much love we put into all of our doing. If you think about it, everything that is involved in parenting—discipline, happiness, self-esteem, emotional intelligence, etc—and in life will fall into place much easier if we practice them first and foremost with real love.

MINDING OUR MAGIC, SHARING OUR SELVES

Everybody knows that a good mother gives her children a feeling of trust and stability. She is their earth. She is the one they can count on for the things that matter most of all. She is their food and their bed and their extra blanket when it grows cold in the night; she is their warmth and their health and their shelter; she is the one they want to be near when they cry. She is the only person in the whole world, or in a whole lifetime, who can be these things to her children. There is no substitute for her.

—Katharine Butler Hathaway, *The Little Locksmith*

There is something magical about us as Moms and women. Our biology and nature give us the power to create, nurture, heal, teach, comfort, unite, protect, and love. Fiercely. We are wired to tend to our children, neighbours and loved ones, to make a home, to maintain peace in our families, to bring people together, and to soothe others in need. And with this power, this gift, comes great wisdom, strength . . . and responsibility. Our children, families, communities, and world need what we have to offer. Why do you think everyone in our home gravitates toward us? We are the ones who get bombarded with requests and complaints, who are sought out to apply Band-Aids, make ponytails and solve relationship troubles, and who are called on at the end of a very long day to be the chief tucker-inner only to retire to the couch and be bombarded by the cat and the dog! We are the hub, the heartbeat of our homes. And we have everything we need to fulfil this responsibility. Our job is to restore our inner resources, reconnect to our inner Selves, and show up.

> **The world needs what women can do. The world needs "mother" to set things right in our unbalanced world.**
>
> —Jean Shinoda Bolen, M.D.

Every Little Thing She Does is Magic

THE MAGICAL EFFECT MOMS HAVE ON OTHERS

Because of the nature of our brain wiring and hormonal make-up, we have an extraordinary ability to comfort and improve the mental, emotional, and physical well-being of the people around us—often without our awareness. Scientists believe that this ability stems from what is called an "affiliative neurocircuitry"—an automatic protective reaction that lowers stress responses such as heart rate, blood pressure, and stress hormones in the people around us.

Research has shown that simply being in our presence has a calming effect on our children, husbands, friends, and even strangers. In fact, in marital relationships, we increase the life expectancy of our husbands by up to 90 percent!

During stressful and non-stressful times across our lifetime, we all benefit from the magic of Mom. So the next time you hear "Mooom," have five people vying for your attention all at once, are engulfed by your crying child, or bombarded by the family dog, remember that you are the one with the magic touch.

Source: Taylor, Shelley E. (2002). The Tending Instinct. *New York: Times Books.*

When we go about our daily lives from a place that is not running on empty, that is centered on mindfulness, acceptance, compassion, and appreciation—for both Self and others—we shift from sacrificing to purposeful giving. This kind of giving does not deplete our inner resources the way mindless doing and striving does. As Anne Morrow Lindbergh points out in *Gift from the Sea*, purposeful giving "belongs to that natural order of giving that seems to renew itself even in the act of depletion. The more one gives, the more one has to give."

But this, too, is not easy. This kind of giving is invisible, without tangible results or pay raises from the boss. It often goes unnoticed and unappreciated. We often feel like thankless servants rather than honored mothers. And where is the purpose in that? It is far easier to try to find purposefulness and a feeling of indispensability in careers, projects, and activities where there are immediate and tangible results. But unless we come at these things from a place that is already in a state of self-acceptance and self-appreciation, we will continue to search outside ourselves—fruitlessly—for that sense of value and purpose that is missing. We will continue to run on empty because we are looking for something to get rather than looking to give what we already have.

People spend their lifetimes trying to find their "purpose." What am I meant to be doing? What is my sole purpose in life? Why am I here? Like passion, we think about purpose with a capital "P," like some kind of grand phenomenon that requires years of search and discovery. That once discovered will tell us exactly what we're supposed to do. But our purpose is right in front of us, all the time, and is not concerned with what we *do*. It has little to do with a title, occupation, place, or project. Our purpose is found each moment as we choose to be who we really are and share that with others. It doesn't matter whether you're a waitress or a CEO, a stay-at-home Mom, a teacher, or a doctor. If you have children, a husband, family, friends, neighbors, co-workers, clients, customers,

> You don't have to go looking for love when it's where you come from.
>
> —WERNER ERHARD

and Self, you have a purpose. The question is: Are you being true to your Self? Are you using your unique qualities, talents, and genius in ways that add to the quality of life of the people around you? Are you sharing love rather than fear and judgment in your world? As physician of the heart Gordon Livingston asks in his book, *How to Love*: "If you were arrested for love, would there be enough evidence to convict?"

The Mommy Diaries

PAYING IT FORWARD

I've learned the value of stripping motherhood down to the basics: love, respect, compassion, stillness, to be attentive, to be able to absorb the moment. I've learned this from the amazing women who came before me—my mother and my grandmother. I remember how present my grandmother was—how she always had time to listen to me and share stories I loved to hear about her childhood. I remember making sandwiches and cake with my mother to take to a neighbor who had lost her husband. I remember the simplicity of these women and how they touched other people with their kindness. To actively attempt to be a good mother is basically attempting to be a good person—to be loving, kind, compassionate, respectful, and present. It's the cycle that keeps going forward. I give those things to my kids, so they can pass them on to their kids. You have to be delighted by that.

Andie, Mom of two and fashion designer

When we connect with the healthiest parts of ourselves and put that out into the world, we find ourselves "on purpose." Life does not become perfect. We don't become martyrs and give up everything in the name of love and motherhood. Our bullshit trackers are still in check. But life does become more authentic, joyful, and meaningful. We become who we are meant to be. In doing so, we pass on a legacy to our children of what it means to be in this world: to feel deeply and love fiercely; to be both soft and powerful; to have faith when things look hopeless; to be both practical and spiritual; and to offer ourselves to others without concern for what we'll receive in return. The mystical poet Hafiz of Shiraz articulated this beautifully when he said, *"Even after all this time the sun never says to the earth, "you owe me." Look what*

You will find as you look back upon your life that the moments when you have really lived are the moments when you have done things in the spirit of love.

—HENRY DRUMMOND

161

happens with a love like that. It lights the whole sky." This is the art of loving and purposeful giving at its ultimate.

* * * * *

Your children, your family, your community, and the world need what you have to offer. And you have everything you need. Your essential nature *is* love; *is* significance, *is* openness and presence; *is* softness and strength; *is* beauty and intelligence; *is* richness and generosity. You only have to connect with it . . . then pass it on.

REFLECTION AND ACTION FOR PATH SEVEN

- In what ways can you infuse more love into your daily doing? Where do you find yourself functioning on automatic pilot and rote love? Make a conscious commitment when you wake up in the morning to show up for your day "on purpose" with more presence, mindfulness, tolerance, and appreciation. When you catch yourself on auto pilot—rushing mindlessly to get onto something else, being impatient and quick to anger or judge, or taking someone for granted—bring your attention back to the present moment and bring love into the situation.

- Many Moms find it easy to give attention, nurturance, affection, and appreciation to others, but have a very difficult time receiving it in return. How easy is it for you to receive love? Like gratitude, love is a revolving door—it must go out from our hearts and come back in to nourish us physically, emotionally, and spiritually. Remember that you, as much as anyone, deserve your love and affection.

- Consider what you have learned from the women who came before you—your mother and grandmothers. What did they teach you about respect, compassion, honoring others, and being a loving presence in the world? Next, consider the legacy you are passing on to your children, especially if you have a daughter who will one day be the mother that follows you. What do you want your children to learn from you? Amidst our busy, hectic lives saturated with TV, movies, video games and social media, are you taking the time to pass on the wisdom your children need to offer their loving presence to the world?

FURTHER READING FOR PATH SEVEN

Handbook for the Heart: Original Writings on Love by Richard Carlson and Benjamin Shield (New York: Little, Brown & Company, 1996)

This book offers 34 original essays from celebrated contemporary writers and experts in the fields of spirituality and healing. The central theme of the book is love—what it is and how we can nurture and express it in our everyday lives. A delightful, inspiring read.

True Love: A Practice for Awakening the Heart by Thich Nhat Hanh (Boston: Shambhala Publications, 1997)

In this little treasure, the renowned Zen monk offers timeless wisdom into the nature of real love. With his trademark warmth and simplicity, he explores the key aspects of love as described in the Buddhist tradition and offers simple techniques for experiencing real love in our everyday lives.

A Return to Love: Reflections on the Principles in "A Course in Miracles" by Marianne Williamson (New York: HarperCollins, 1992)

A classic spiritual guide, Williamson offers her reflections on *A Course in Miracles* and her insights on how practicing love is the key to inner peace, making our own lives more fulfilling and creating a more peaceful and loving world for our children.

Part Three

Staying the Path

OKAY, NOW WHAT?

Taking the Next Step

It is said that knowledge is power, but knowledge that lies dormant in your brain will not move your life forward. It's what you do with what you know that will make the difference in your life. The moment your brain sends the message "Move" to your feet is the moment when you walk across the bridge and change your life forever. What will it take for you to finally act? . . . Take the step—the bridge will be there.

—GRACE CIROCO, *Take the Step: The Bridge Will Be There*

Believe me. I know what happens at this point of a self-help book. You've taken in a lot of information, you're feeling inspired to live differently (well, hopefully you are!), and you're thinking, "Okay, this all sounds great, but now what?" Having read through seven reinvention pathways, you may be feeling overwhelmed; that all of the suggestions and ideas in the book are just too much. You don't know where to start, don't have the time or energy, or feel like it's too much work. Or maybe it seems too difficult and you don't have the support you need to take the journey. Whatever the case may be, the book tends to go on a shelf and life, along with running on empty, goes on. Please don't let that happen. This chapter will give you the tools and confidence you need to take the next step beyond this book and allow reinvention to be a new beginning in your life.

Having read this far, there's nothing left to do but take a step. It doesn't have to be *the* step. It doesn't have to be a specially planned, measurable, or time-sensitive step. It just has to be *a* step. It may be the journey of a thousand miles, but it all begins with that single step. This is how we commit to the journey. In that commitment, we continue to connect to our inner selves, to the people in our lives, and to what matters most to us. And as we

The greatest of all mistakes is to do nothing because you can only do a little. Do what you can.

—LIZ SMITH

travel the journey with commitment and connection, we remember to celebrate along the way. These three C's—commit, connect, and celebrate—are the focus of this chapter.

COMMIT

I know what you're thinking. This is the part where I give the big motivational speech filled with clichés about living your best life and being epic. That if you commit to reinventing your life by exercising three times a week and eating healthier, by getting up a half hour earlier to take quiet time for yourself and write in your journal, by dedicating one hour each week to clearing out the emotional and physical clutter in your life, and by looking for ways to find enchantment and love every day, you'll be a better Mom and a better you. After all, this is the improvement formula we are used to: the stronger you commit, the harder you work, the more and faster you will achieve. But that is the old way, the way that leads to running on empty. I can feel the weariness and exhaustion in just writing all of those commitments. Nope. This is not the part where we jump up shouting, "Let's do it!" light our bras on fire, and march headstrong into the Mom Revolution. We're done with that way. In committing to the reinvention journey, I'm simply asking you to quietly say, "Yes" and walk with me.

> No trumpets sound when the important decisions of our life are made. Destiny is made known silently.
>
> —Agnes de Mille

Once you say yes, committing involves looking back on the reinvention pathways and choosing the path that resonated with you the most. Which of the seven themes seems most applicable to where you are in your life right now? Stuck in low energy and fatigue? Path Two may be a good place to start. Are you overwhelmed with emotional clutter? Try Path Three. Or maybe you feel stuck in your left brain, disconnected from feeling? Try starting at Path One. If you've already started practices in one of the pathways while you were reading, stick with that path for now. And if one particular area doesn't resonate with you, start at the first pathway or choose one randomly. The point is to choose *one* path and *one* practice within that path and begin there. Don't think about the thousands of steps you see ahead of you. Focus on that first step and tell your feet to move.

Looking back on my own journey of reinvention, I marvel at how what started with the simple yearning for "something more" transpired into seven different pathways of learning and growth. I can't help but think that if I had seen a breakdown of how much there was to learn and all the steps I would continue to take, I probably would have gone back to bed. In many ways, motherhood is not much different. Let's be honest. If we had seen a breakdown of all the challenges, tough decisions, emotional turmoil, sleepless nights, tantrums, time, costs, and learning associated with having a family, most of us would have seriously reconsidered the parenting route. Of course, hindsight is always 20/20 and knowing what we know now about the sheer love, joy, and enchantment that our children and family bring to our lives, we wouldn't have done it any other way. But it's also important to recognize that we went into parenthood with a beginner's mind. Without knowing all the specific details about what we were getting into, we were able to deal with things and learn what we needed to know on an "as needed" basis. And so it is with the reinvention journey. If you can commit to the journey with a beginner's mind, without worrying about all the pathways, learning and steps to take, and simply take one step at a time, you open up your life to many opportunities for wisdom, love, and joy.

As you begin walking that first pathway, reflecting on the ideas and insights and engaging in the reinvention practices, you'll start to feel the difference in your life. And as you keep putting one foot in front of the other, you'll start to see how that pathway unfolds into another pathway and then another. Step by step, your life as a Mom and woman will unfold in wonderful ways.

CONNECT

Because our lives can get so busy and outward-focused, maintaining connection is a cornerstone in staying the reinvention path. I have found throughout the course of my own journey that staying connected in the following three areas helps tremendously along the way . . .

Feelings

Remember that our feelings are our inner compass. They are the manifestation of our inner voice and are our direct line to Self. They are our guiding companions on this journey . . . if you listen. As you continue to pay attention and learn to listen to and embrace your feelings, it will become easier to heed their messages with confidence.

One of the biggest ways your feelings will assist you is by giving you warning signals about running on empty creeping in. The more you tune in and respond to those signals, the easier it will become to shift out of the downward spiral that ensues. As we know from Path Three on clearing out emotional clutter, some of our feeling work involves time and healing—it's an ongoing process. However, there will be moments and days when our feelings signal that we are running on empty and we can respond accordingly in those moments. The following chart outlines how you can shift from those low, stagnant levels to higher, healthier levels of energy and feeling. While referring to a chart may seem a little awkward and inconvenient, know that in time you will be able to identify and make these shifts readily in your own mind.

When You Feel	You Can . . .
Fatigued, Sluggish	Slow down. Tune in to your hormonal balance and physical needs. Let go of the need to get it all done. Ask for help. Take a break.
Overwhelmed, Frazzled	Stop and breathe. Connect to the present moment. Tune in to your hormonal balance and physical needs. Identify what you can say "no" to. Ask for help; let others know what you need. Let go of the need to get it all done.
Depressed	Tune in to your hormonal balance and physical needs. Accept the feelings. Find quiet space to reflect on what's missing or not working. Connect or set an intention to connect with what you really want. If feelings are purely hormonal, know that this too shall pass.
Worried, Fearful	Connect to the present moment. Tune in to your hormonal balance and physical needs. Identify what you can control and let go of the need to control everything else. Trust that things will work out and unfold the way they need to. Recite the Serenity Prayer.
Guilty	Identify what went wrong—Did you make a mistake? Are your expectations unrealistic? Identify what you can do differently—Change your behavior? Change your thoughts and expectations? Apologize to someone if necessary. Let go of the need for perfection. Forgive yourself.
Impatient	Stop and breathe. Connect to the present moment. Choose a kinder, more loving response. Tune in to your hormonal balance and physical needs. Let go of the need to be in control.

When You Feel	You Can . . .
Angry, Stuck in Pissosity	Stop and breathe.
	Let go of the need to be right.
	Tune in to your hormonal balance and physical needs.
	Forgive.
	Practice compassion and speak to the other person in a way you would want to be spoken to under the circumstance.
	Communicate your feelings when you are in a calmer place.
Judgmental	Recognize that you are creating toxic energy.
	Put yourself in the other person's shoes and try to understand he/she is doing the best they know how at the time.
	Choose a kinder, more tolerant response.
Lonely	Find quiet time for yourself to reflect on what you need.
	Find ways to connect meaningfully with others.
	Remember everyone who loves you and all you have to be grateful for.
Inadequate	Speak kindly to yourself, the same way you would to your child.
	Let go of the need to compare yourself to others.
	Know that you are always enough.
Unappreciated	Examine your expectations.
	Let go of your "shoulds."
	Find quiet time for yourself to explore what you truly need.
	Do something nice for someone.

Remember that staying true to our feelings also involves staying connected to our bullshit tracker. We know how easy it is to get stuck in feeling, to become overwhelmed and/or confused by emotion, so tuning in to our trackers is important for keeping us connected to what is real and *what is*. It allows us to turnaround thoughts and self-talk that keep us stuck in running on empty and do not serve us or our families. *"No one EVER looks after my needs." "I'm a terrible mother." "I'm so tired. Why do I get stuck doing everything?"* When we get stuck in these mind-sets, we can remember the "Shifting Focus" practice from Path Six. We can ask ourselves, "Is this thought 100% undeniably true?" When we recognize that there is no evidence for our thinking, we can call out the B.S. and move on to what works.

The Mommy Diaries

CALLING MYSELF OUT

Growing up, my family used to play a card game called "Bullshit!" (It's also known as "I Don't Think So," "Cheat" and "No Way.") Players try to get rid of their cards through deceptive card playing and it's up to the other players to yell "Bullshit!" to call out a player on his/her bluff.

It's funny. I haven't played the game in years, but I often find myself as a wife and mother trying to get rid of built up stress and negative feelings by complaining and being short-tempered with my family. When I catch myself doing this I often yell "Bullshit!" in my own mind to call out my "deceptive" behavior. As soon as I call myself out, it's like a wake up call that allows me to get on with things in a real way. It may sound strange, but it works!

Kim, Mom of three and charity fundraiser

Friends

Success occurs in community. One of the most powerful forces that will help you stay the reinvention path is a friend or group of like-minded Moms who are also on the journey. Creating safe and nurturing communities is part of who we are as Moms and women—we are meant to reach out and support one another rather than remain alone and isolated in our thoughts and feelings as we often do. When we connect in the spirit of trust, respect, creativity, and partnership, we establish what writer and artist Julia Cameron calls "a believing mirror" for ourselves.

> **I envision a world filled with women traveling alone and meeting each other along the path.**
> —S.A.R.K., *Succulent Wild Woman*

A believing mirror is a partner or group of friends who believes in you and your reinvention journey. As Moms, we can create a circle of believing mirrors to help actualize each other's growth and reflect a "yes you can" to the steps each of us takes along the way.

A Mom's group, online community, or partnership with a sister or friend, are a few ways you can connect with a circle of believing mirrors. Once you have at least one other person to partner with, you can put a plan in place to work together. Appendix B offers ideas and guidelines you might find helpful in forming a reinvention circle.

Whatever form your circle happens to take, it's important to ensure it is built on the cornerstones of trust, respect, compassion, and generosity . . .

Reinvention will flourish in a place that is a safe haven, where there is a high level of *trust* and acceptance, where Moms can openly share their feelings and insights, be vulnerable, take risks, ask for help, and receive constructive feedback. Criticism, judgment, blame, sarcasm, gossip, and other energies that diminish trust and acceptance, have no place in the circle.

Respect and *compassion* are essential for honoring everyone in the circle. Each person will be at different points along the path and will travel at different paces and in different ways. It's important that Moms honor and respect each other and their differences along the journey.

Reinvention grows in *generosity*—generosity of mind, heart, and spirit. Success occurs when everyone comes to the circle with an open mind, a compassionate heart, and a willingness to share. We are all teachers with gifts, knowledge, and experience that we can pass on to help others. When we take the time to share our personal experiences, be a believing mirror, and offer our support in the spirit of friendship and community, we all help each other navigate the paths of motherhood and womanhood together.

Friendship is born at that moment when one person says to another, "What! You too? I thought I was the only one."

—C.S. Lewis

"Know this well," says Julia Cameron. "Success occurs in clusters and is born in generosity. Let us form constellations of believing mirrors and move into our powers." Amen.

Faith

You likely recall that the topic of faith was discussed in Path Six on the art of letting go, but it is such an important ingredient for our journey that I wanted to include it again in this final chapter. As you travel the reinvention pathways, there will be moments. Moments of anger and frustration where things aren't going the way you thought they would, or should; moments of despair where you can't imagine how you'll go on; moments of worry and fear where you don't know how you'll make things work; moments of defeat where you'll feel like nothing's working, so why bother. In those moments, faith is moving forward anyway knowing that there will be something to sustain you; knowing, as *A Course in Miracles* reminds us, that "All things work together for good," even if it seems impossible to understand at the time.

There will be many unknowns along this journey. Scary? Hell yes. But the thing is, as you continue to face those unknowns and realize that you can handle whatever shows up, all of these unknowns start to become kind of exciting. Because in addition to all of the not-so-pleasant unknowns come a whole lot of wonderful

Fear can keep us up all night long, but faith makes one fine pillow.

—ANONYMOUS

unknowns, too—a surprise package in the mail, an unexpected offer or accolade, a moment of enchantment, a hidden opportunity, a pregnancy or even multiple pregnancy! The comedian and actress Gilda Radner calls this "delicious ambiguity." As you learn to embrace this ambiguity and trust in yourself and that force, that divine flow that is greater than yourself, without attachment to how things turn out, you will move forward with confidence, courage, and grace.

And when faced with uncertainties, frustrations, and worries that don't feel particularly delicious in the moment, the following insight from poet Patrick Overton is one that keeps me connected to faith. Unequivocally.

When you have come to the edge
Of all light that you know
And are about to step off into the darkness
Of the unknown,
Faith is knowing
One of two things will happen:
There will be something solid to stand on or
You will be taught to fly.

CELEBRATE

I know how easy it is on the journey to get caught up in focusing on *"there."* You want to get to that place where you experience more energy, wisdom, and joy. You want to know who you are as a unique individual so you can share that with others. *Now.* And so we set our goals and jump into action to make things happen. But remember this: *There* is never better than *here.* Whenever we get to our there, we simply find another there to reach for. This is the old way of creating change and making things happen. Not us. We're sinking into this life, connecting to what matters most, and embracing the delicious ambiguity of it all. And we're going to celebrate along the way.

Celebrating is such a powerful way to connect with life and the present moment. It's a doorway to enchantment. If you think about some of your strongest memories, many of them most likely involve a celebration of some kind—the birth of your baby, your wedding day, a graduation or milestone, a family reunion. In the same spirit, take time to celebrate your successes along this journey—big and small. Do you have more energy? Did you clear out some long-lingering emotional clutter? Were you able to show love and patience in a moment where you normally would have snapped? Have you discovered something about your Self? Or maybe you just made it through "one of those days." There is so much to celebrate along the way if you keep your heart open and your head in the moment. Honor yourself by taking time to reflect on and acknowledge how far you've come.

Most importantly, as you commit to the journey, lighten up and enjoy this time. This is your life and these are your children, so connect with what matters most to you and savor the moments—on your own terms and in your unique way. As Abraham-Hicks reminds us, "Every single activity that you're involved in is for one purpose only, and that is to give you a moment of joy. Lighten up. Laugh more. Appreciate more. All is well."

*   *   *   *   *

"We're always afraid to start something that we want to make very good, true and serious," says writer Brenda Ueland. This is so true when it comes to reinvention and becoming the Moms and women we're meant to be. Indeed, life, motherhood, and our children are very good, true, and serious. But don't overthink or overplan your journey. And please don't put this book away. You have everything you need. Just say yes. Say yes. Show up. And walk with me.

**"It's impossible," said pride.
"It's risky," said experience.
"It's pointless," said reason.
"Give it a try," whispered heart.**

—Anonymous

Quiz: Are You an Innie or an Outie?
Discovering Your Personal Energy Type

According to psychological theory, there are two ways people get personal energy—either by engaging in the outer world of people and activities (the extrovert or "outie" type) or by engaging in their inner world of ideas and experiences (the introvert or "innie" type). Whether you're an introverted, innie type or an extraverted, outie type is very much like right- and left-handedness—there isn't a right or wrong preference. Life just tends to go more smoothly and efficiently when you can engage in your preferred way of doing things. In this way, knowing your emotional energy type will go a long way in helping you understand and manage your energy on a regular basis. Here are some questions to help you determine your personal energy type . . .

For each of the following statements, select the preference that reflects "the real you." In other words, which would be your first choice based on what feels most comfortable to you, not what you think you should be or want to be?

1) Do you consider yourself:

    a.   a good listener
    b.   a good talker

2) At a social gathering, do you tend to:

    a.   interact with a few friends
    b.   interact with many, even strangers

3) When working on a project, do you prefer to:

    a. work on your own
    b. work in a group or committee

4) In general, do you find being busy and on-the-go:

    a. exhausting
    b. energizing

5) When making a decision do you prefer to:

    a. take time to think about it
    b. make a quick decision on the spot

6) On a Friday night, would you prefer to:

    a. spend quiet time with your family
    b. invite friends and neighbors over for a get-together

7) People would most likely describe you as:

    a. quiet and reserved
    b. lively and outgoing

8) When it comes to birthday parties, do you prefer to plan:

    a. something small scale with a few close friends and family
    b. a big event with lots of people, food, and activities

9) When meeting new people, would you say:

    a. it takes a while to get to know you; you tend to share personal information only with those close to you
    b. it's easy to know you; you share information about yourself and your family openly and easily

10) At your kids sporting events and activities, do you tend to:

    a.   sit back and take everything in
    b.   cheer loudly and get involved

11) If you were given an entire weekend to yourself, you would most likely:

    a.   curl up with a good book or movie at home and relish the time alone
    b.   call up your girlfriends and plan a girls' weekend of fun

TOTAL

_____ a. statements

_____ b. statements

Count how many a and b statements you selected. If you chose more a statements, you are an introverted, innie type and tend to get your energy from internal sources. If you chose more b statements, you are an extraverted, outie type who gets her energy from external sources.

As you begin to recognize the differences between introverts and extraverts, it will become much easier to accept and respect your personal type, as well as those of others, including your children. You can replenish your emotional energy more readily; you'll feel far less guilty about your needs; and you'll be able to maintain higher levels of energy for the things that matter most.

Appendix B

Forming a Mom Reinvention Circle

In creating a reinvention community or partnership with like-minded Moms, I know you'll find that your life will change in wonderful, unexpected ways. The support, friendship, wisdom, and strength you'll gain from fellow Moms will encourage you to tune in to your feelings, bring your deepest longings into being, and be more of the Mom and woman you want and are meant to be. The following sections offer ideas for starting and running a great Mom reinvention circle in your area. Good luck!

> **Women meeting in groups creates an energy that is very power-full.**
>
> —S.A.R.K., *Succulent Wild Woman*

STARTING A CIRCLE

More and more Moms today are finding community with like-minded women in on-line forums. This is a great way to connect and find support with fellow Moms on your own time and in the comfort of your own home. Starting an on-line group is as simple as finding a community on an established website for women and mothers and creating a sub-group for Moms interested in reinvention.

If you can, a face-to-face community is a richer, more intimate environment for reinvention. Although it is not as convenient as an on-line community, the benefits of the face-to-face interaction and personal contact with fellow Moms are immeasurable. The following section outlines ideas for forming a circle meeting-in-person.

When you are enlisting new members, keep in mind that six to eight people is most productive for this type of community. Having said that, don't wait until you have that many. Once you have at least one other Mom, get started and add new members as they come. Also be sure that interested Moms are clear on the intention for the group: to support one another in learning and growing in our lives as Moms and women.

RUNNING A SUCCESSFUL CIRCLE

Since the intention is to create a community of support, encouragement, growth, and friendship, it's important for your group to meet regularly. I suggest getting together weekly, bi-weekly, or monthly and going through the exercises in the book together, sharing insights and challenges each of you has experienced. This practice not only provides reassurance and normalizes our shared experiences, but also reveals insights that can trigger breakthroughs for others in the circle.

To participate, each Mom only needs the commitment to the reinvention journey, to attend the group meetings, and to follow the group guidelines . . .

Guiding Principles for the Circle

Having guiding principles in place will help ensure the success of your community by creating an open, safe space and for avoiding the kinds of habits that can derail a group. You might consider refining and/or adding to these guidelines for your particular group and making copies available for each member.

- *Commit to Confidentiality.* What happens in the group, stays in the group. In order to maintain a safe, trusting space where members can be open and vulnerable with their feelings and experiences, everything that is said in the circle is to be held in strict confidence.
- *Listen and Speak from the Heart.* Speak from your own experience and feelings (e.g., using "I" rather than "you" statements) rather than offering unsolicited advice or "shoulds." Listen with an open mind and a compassionate heart rather than with judgment or criticism. Remember that we all do the best we can with what have and know in the moment and we're all at different points along the path carrying different sets of baggage.
- *Speak One at a Time and Give Each Person an Equal Chance to be Heard.* Ensure that each member of the group is given equal time to speak and be heard. There will be occasions when a fellow Mom may be going through a difficult time and will need extra attention, but in general, it's important to prevent individuals from continuously dominating the conversation. In the event a member of the circle comes to each meeting stuck on the same issue without taking action to move forward, this person may need more individualized support from a mental health professional such as a counselor or physician. Do the loving thing by being honest and offering to help this Mom get the support she needs.
- *Be Responsible for the Energy You Bring into the Space.* Ensure that your presence in and contributions to the group are positive. Focus on what works, find ways to acknowledge others' strengths and wisdom, celebrate successes, and minimize complaining.

❀ *Share Leadership and Responsibilities.* Take turns leading/facilitating the circle each time you meet to prevent those with natural leader, teacher, or caretaker tendencies from taking over. This is important to ensure everyone in the group gets the support they need.

❀ *Honor the Group.* Decide together how decisions will be made and work together to address any issues or problems that arise. For example, you might check in at the end of each meeting to address any ideas, feedback, or concerns members may have. If there are any issues (e.g., someone is dominating the discussion or disregarding the circle guidelines), tell the truth about how you feel in a constructive way.

Circle Format and Facilitation

Be creative with the format you use for your circle. Some groups may want to gather while each member walks their own pathway in their own way, while other groups might form around a specific pathway and travel the journey together. For example, a circle may form around the female fizziology pathway and Moms would support each other in improving the food, fitness, and flow in their lives. Once everyone has agreed upon the format, here are some ideas for facilitating each gathering:

1. *Leading/Facilitating*: Take turns leading/facilitating the circle. The facilitator is responsible for keeping the group focused and on time, ensuring each person has equal time to speak and that only one person speaks at a time, and redirecting any tangents or complain fests that go on for too long. We all need to digress and rant from time to time, but when it goes on too long (e.g., more than a minute or two) it becomes unproductive for both the individual and the group. Some groups find it helpful to use a timer or buzzer in a fun way to signal when a digression or rant has exceeded its time!

2. *Opening*: Begin with 10-15 minutes of sharing news, catching up, or letting go of anything that might prevent you from being fully present. You might consider having someone segue into the discussion portion of the meeting with a quote, prayer, story, or exercise to shift everyone's energy and attention into a positive, loving space. This role should be assigned in advance of the gathering.

3. *Group Discussion*: Ensure each Mom has equal time to speak. Allow the first person to speak without interruption for the allotted time about her reactions to a pathway, any practices she tried, or areas where she feels stuck or confused. When each Mom is finished, allow her to ask for feedback and/or support from the circle. Challenge her to be specific about her needs and in asking for help. Each Mom then commits to her action steps for the next gathering before moving on to the next person.

4. *Closing*: Once each member has had a chance to be fully heard, give Moms the opportunity to ask for and receive or offer any additional help or feedback. Address any issues or ideas

collectively as a group. The facilitator can then fill roles and responsibilities for the next gathering (e.g., facilitator/leader, etc). Finally, you might consider having the facilitator or other assigned member end the meeting with an inspirational quote, poem, or prayer as a departing thought.

Finally, remember to celebrate and have fun! While you are all there to support and encourage one another in being the Moms and women you're meant to be, it's just as important to lighten up, laugh, and appreciate one another. Bring in a guest to lead a fun, unique session one week. Yoga? Tarot Card reader? Masseuse? Plan a GNO (girls night out) where you can all let go and have fun together for an evening. Be creative. Celebrate. And have fun as you journey the pathways of motherhood together.

REFERENCES

Albion, Mark. *More Than Money: Questions Every MBA Needs to Answer: Redefining Risk and Reward for a Life of Purpose.* San Francisco: BK Life, 2008.

Albion, Mark. *The Good Life* (video). Oakland: Free Range Studios, 2008.

Amen, Daniel G. *Change Your Brain, Change Your Life.* New York: Three Rivers Press, 1999.

American Psychological Association. "Stress and Gender." In *Press Release: Stress in America, January 1, 2011.* Washington, DC: American Psychological Association. http://www.apa.org/news/press/releases/stress/gender-stress.pdf.

Ban Breathnach, Sarah. *Simple Abundance: A Daybook of Comfort and Joy.* New York: Warner Books, 1995.

Brizendine, Louann. *The Female Brain.* London: Bantam Press, 2007.

Carlson, Richard and Shield, Benjamin (Eds.). *Handbook for the Heart: Original Writings on Love.* New York: Little, Brown & Company, 1996.

Cirocco, Grace. *Take the Step—The Bridge Will Be There: Inspiration and Guidance for Moving Your Life Forward.* Toronto: HarperCollins Publishers Canada, 2001.

Colbert, Don. *Deadly Emotions: Understand the Mind-Body-Spirit Connection that Can Heal or Destroy You.* Nashville: Thomas Nelson, 2006.

Cole, Julie. "Mrs. Judgy McJudgerson at the Mall." YummyMummyClub.ca Blog, March 1, 2011. Toronto: Erica Ehm Communications. http://www.yummymummyclub.ca/blogs/julie-cole-the-baby-machine/mrs-judgy-mcjudgerson-at-the-mall.

Crenshaw, Dave. *The Myth of Multitasking: How Doing It All Gets Nothing Done.* New York: Jossey-Bass, 2008.

De Angelis, Barbara. *Passion.* New York: Dell, 1999.

Dyer, Wayne W. *Living the Wisdom of the Tao: The Complete Tao Te Ching and Affirmations.* Carlsbad, CA: Hay House, 2008.

Dyer, Wayne W. *Manifest Your Destiny: The Nine Spiritual Principles for Getting Everything You Want.* New York: HarperPaperbacks, 1999.

Dyer, Wayne W. *There's a Spiritual Solution to Every Problem.* New York: HarperCollins, 2001.

Friedan, Betty. *The Feminine Mystique.* New York: W.W. Norton & Company, 1963.

Gaudet, Tracy W. *Consciously Female: How to Listen to Your Body and Your Soul for a Lifetime of Healthier Living.* New York: Random House, 2004.

Gilbert, Elizabeth. *Eat, Pray, Love: One Woman's Search for Everything Across Italy, India and Indonesia.* New York: Penguin Books, 2006.

Greene, Robert A. and Feldon, Leah. *Dr. Robert Greene's Perfect Balance.* New York: Three Rivers Press, 2005.

Gurian, Michael. *The Wonder of Girls: Understanding the Hidden Nature of Our Daughters.* New York: Atria Books, 2002.

Hanh, Thich Nhat. *True Love: A Practice for Awakening the Heart.* Boston: Shambhala Publications, 1997.

Hathaway, Katherine Butler. *The Little Locksmith.* New York: Coward-McCann, 1943.

Hay, Louise. *You Can Heal Your Life.* Carlsbad, CA: Hay House, 1984.

Hosseini, Khaled. *The Kite Runner.* New York: Riverhead Trade, 2004.

Institute of HeartMath. *Science of the Heart.* Boulder Creek: Institute of HeartMath, 2001.

Johnson, Robert A. *We: Understanding the Psychology of Romantic Love.* New York: HarperOne, 1985.

Katie, Byron. *Loving What Is: Four Questions That Can Change Your Life.* New York: Three Rivers Press, 2003.

Kidd, Sue Monk. *When the Heart Waits.* New York: HarperCollins, 1990.

Koff, Ashley and Kaehler, Kathy. *Mom Energy: A Simple Plan to Live Fully Charged* Carlsbad, CA: Hay House, 2011.

Kogan, Lisa. "The Truth About Mommy Time." In *Live Your Best Life: A Treasury of Wisdom, Wit, Advice, Interviews, and Inspiration from O, The Oprah Magazine.* Birmingham: Oxmoor House, 2005.

Lindbergh, Anne Morrow. *Gift from the Sea.* New York: Pantheon Books, 1955.

Livingston, Gordon. *How to Love: Choosing Well at Every Stage of Life.* New York: Dacapo Press, 2011.

Lundin, Mia. *Female Brain Gone Insane.* Deerfield Beach: Health Communications, Inc., 2009.

Mental Health America. *Maternal Depression: Making a Difference Through Community Action, December 2008.* Alexandria, VA: Mental Health America. http://www.mentalhealthamerica. net/maternal_depression_guide.pdf.

Mountain Dreamer, Oriah. *The Invitation.* New York: HarperOne, 1999.

Mountain Dreamer, Oriah. *The Call: Discovering Why You Are Here.* New York: HarperOne, 2003.

Myss, Caroline. *Anatomy of the Spirit: The Seven Stages of Power and Healing.* New York: Three Rivers Press, 1996.

Nachmanovitch, Stephen. *Free Play: The Power of Improvisation in Life and the Arts.* New York: Jeremy P. Tarcher/Perigree Books, 1990.

Northrup, Christiane. *Women's Bodies, Women's Wisdom.* New York: Bantam Dell, 2006.

Nouwen, Henri. *Spiritual Direction: Wisdom for the Long Walk of Faith.* New York: HarperOne, 2006.

Pearsall, Paul. *The Heart's Code.* New York: Broadway Books, 1999.

Pearson, Allison. *I Don't Know How She Does It.* New York: Alfred A. Knopf, 2002.

Pink, Daniel. *A Whole New Mind: Why Right Brainers Will Rule The World.* New York: Riverhead Books, 2006.

Richards, Dick. *Setting Your Genius Free.* New York: Berkley Trade, 1998

Richardson, Cheryl. *Finding Your Passion (Audio CD).* Carlsbad, CA: Hay House, 2002.

Robbins, Jhan and June. "Why Young Mothers Feel Trapped." Redbook, Sept. 1960.

Schucman, Helen. *A Course in Miracles.* New York: Viking: The Foundation for Inner Peace, 1996

Schulz, Mona Lisa. *Awakening Intuition: Using Your Mind-Body Network for Insight and Healing.* New York: Three Rivers Press, 1999

Schulz, Mona Lisa. *The New Feminine Brain: Developing Your Intuitive Genius.* New York: Free Press, 2005.

Schulz, Mona Lisa. *The Intuitive Advisor.* Carlsbad, CA: Hay House, 2010.

Siegel, Bernie. "Heart Lessons." In R. Carlson and B. Shield (Eds.), *Handbook for the Heart* (pp. 163-169). New York: Little Brown & Company, 1996.

Taylor, Jill Bolte. *My Stroke of Insight: A Brain Scientist's Personal Journey.* New York: Viking, 2006.

Taylor, Shelley E. *The Tending Instinct: Women, Men, and the Biology of Our Relationships.* New York: Times Books, 2002.

Thurer, Shari. *The Myths of Motherhood: How Culture Reinvents the Good Mother.* New York: Penguin, 1995.

Tolle, Eckhart. *A New Earth: Awakening to Your Life's Purpose.* New York: Penguin, 2008.

Vanderhaeghe, Lorna. *A Smart Woman's Guide to Hormones.* Toronto: Fitzhenry and Whiteside, 2011.

Warner, Judith. *Perfect Madness: Motherhood in the Age of Anxiety.* New York: Penguin Group, 2006.

ABOUT THE AUTHOR

Kelly Pryde, Ph.D. is a parent coach and family mediator who has worked with parents, children, and families for more than 20 years. In addition to holding a Ph.D. in Psychology with specialties in behavioral neuroscience and child development, Kelly has completed advanced training in family mediation with renowned mediator Barbara Landau. She is a member of the Ontario Association for Family Mediation (OAFM) and a candidate for the Advanced Certificate in Conflict Resolution from Conrad Grebel's Peace and Conflict Studies Institute at the University of Waterloo.

Kelly writes and teaches regularly on the topics of parenthood, relationships, and child development. Her award-winning research on child learning and development has been published in numerous international journals and her parenting and personal development articles have appeared in both regional and national magazines. She has also appeared as a parenting expert on local television programs and at national parenting shows.

As a wife and mother of two, Kelly knows firsthand the challenges that come with marriage and parenthood in today's fast-paced world. Each requires hard work and can be fraught with difficulties related to communication and emotional turbulence such as guilt, overwhelm, frustration, and "running on empty." A large part of her practice is devoted to helping parents successfully navigate these challenges to be more of the Moms and Dads they want to be for themselves and their children.

Known for her compassionate, down-to-earth approach, Kelly combines her personal experience with her background in psychology and her years as an educator and coach to explain concepts and connect with parents in relevant, life-changing ways.

Kelly lives in Toronto, Canada with her husband and their two children. You can visit her online at www.drkellypryde.com.